The
Country
Home

The Country Home

Ellen M. Plante

MetroBooks

An Imprint of Friedman/Fairfax Publishers

Library of Congress Cataloging-in-Publication Data

Plante, Ellen M.
     The country home / by Ellen M. Plante.
          p.   cm.
     Includes bibliographical references and index.
     ISBN 1-56799-528-4
     1. Decoration and ornament, Rustic—United States.   2. Interior
decorations—United States. I. Title.
NK2002.P6   1998
749.2 ' 3—dc21   98—13418

Editors: Francine Hornberger and Reka Simonsen
Art Director: Jeff Batzli
Designer: Kirsten Wehmann Berger
Photography Editor: Amy Talluto
Production Director: Karen Matsu Greenberg
Color separations by Fine Arts Repro House Co., Ltd.
Printed in Italy by Poligrafiche Bolis SpA.

3 5 7 9 10 8 6 4 2

For bulk purchases and special sales, please contact:
Friedman/Fairfax Publishers
Attention: Sales Department
15 West 26th Street
New York, NY 10010
212/685-6610 FAX 212/685-1307

Visit our website:
http://www.metrobooks.com

Dedication

For all those who endeavor to bring country spirit
to their lives and their homes

Acknowledgments

With special thanks to my editors,

Francine Hornberger and Reka Simonsen,

of the Michael Friedman Publishing Group, Inc.

It has been a pleasure, as always.

Contents

What Is a Country Home?

Speak the word "country" and some people think of babbling brooks, a cool, shaded forest, or a field spilling over with wildflowers. Others may conjure up images of Grandmother's old-fashioned kitchen or her big front porch that proved so ideal for spending lazy afternoons. And then there are those who associate country with a crisp autumn morning spent at a flea market, a cup of hot chocolate enjoyed in front of the hearth on a cold winter's eve, or perhaps simply baking bread from scratch.

Country is indeed all this—and so much more. Country today is an attitude, a way of life that embraces the pure and simple and the tried and true. It's an appreciation for timeworn furnishings and humble utilitarian objects that served households of the past. It's a love of the handcrafted items that brought a dash of color, pattern, comfort, and individuality to rooms of long ago. Country is also the desire to live a scaled-back lifestyle that answers our need for casual, simplified comfort. As an added bonus, country has come to symbolize the revival of long-lost arts—everything from gardening with old-fashioned flowers and weaving textiles to baking from scratch and handcrafting furniture.

As an interior design scheme, country has captured our hearts and imaginations for more than twenty years. Actually, one facet of country decorating has been around for a long time: Colonial Revival. America's centennial celebration in 1876 focused renewed interest on the country's past, and the hard-won spirit of freedom and independence gave renewed life to the architectural styles, furniture designs, and decorative accessories of the Colonial period. As a result, from the late 1800s through the early 1900s, country-style rooms were very much in vogue. In fact, the furnishings produced during this revival are often the antiques that grace many of today's country-style homes.

While the Colonial Revival of the early twentieth century centered strong interest on a single period style, today's country decorating differs in that several interpretations of country have emerged as design schemes all their own. From the warm glow

and patina of aged furnishings to the rustic charms of painted surfaces and simple designs, country style has been refined. Perhaps that's what makes country style so appealing: it's not a single look. Rather, country decorating today can reflect specific regional, period, or cultural characteristics. Ethnic diversity contributes subtle beauty to furnishings, textiles, and everyday household objects. Consider, for example, Amish quilts, a Pennsylvania German painted trunk, or the Norwegian folk art of rosemaling (painting furniture with floral designs and inscriptions).

Stretching beyond the confines of American boundaries, other cultural influences have made an impact on today's country home. French country style is a notable favorite in the United States and abroad. Vibrant, nature-inspired hues, simple yet gracious furnishings, and French Provençal print fabrics have been combined for centuries to create a simple, striking, yet comfortable style of decor. In contrast, the English cottage style calls upon pastels and muted shades to enhance vintage furnishings passed from one generation to the next. Chintz-covered sofas and a lion's share of pottery, collectibles, and bric-a-brac fill the English-style home to overflowing. Even religious influences can be found in today's country decorating, in the furnishings and useful objects crafted during the 1800s and early 1900s by the Shaker sect.

As for period designs, the past few centuries have given us Queen Anne, Chippendale, Victorian, and Arts and Crafts furnishings that can all be adapted to the country-style home. And who could forget the Windsor chair? Add to these period designs the rural furniture adaptations and the wallpaper patterns, rugs, and decorative accessories of each era, and there are myriad ways to fashion a country look that draws upon the best of period design.

Above: Bright flowers, Blue Willow china, and a lovely cabinet create a cheery mood in the kitchen.

Handcrafted period furnishings built by master cabinetmakers were naturally costly and time-consuming to produce, so it's no wonder that our inventive forebears put industry to work in turning out machine-made items that also blend beautifully into today's country-style home. Wicker is especially popular in creating a country Victorian look, while golden oak furnishings recall the style of the rural American farmhouse.

A perfect example of regional country adaptation can be found in the rustic twig furnishings and "camp" look that has developed a strong following in recent years. The quintessential laid-back country look, rustic adaptations have their roots in the great summer camps and lodges of the Adirondacks and the state parks that developed all across America during the early part of the twentieth century. Regional can also refer to the casual style that was born of the American Southwest, with its Native American traditions of adobe buildings, pottery, baskets, and textiles adorned with vibrant geometric patterns.

To say that country decorating has fully developed seems an understatement. What began in the 1970s as a style focusing, for the most part, on primitive (often painted) American furniture pieces, crockery, baskets, and the like, has emerged as a series of country styles that can be sophisticated and casual at the same time. Each variation of country fulfills our need for harmony, comfort, simplicity, and easy style while providing for highly personal expression. With this in mind, *The Country Home* will lead you on a tour of eight different interpretations of country style.

Above: Colorful pillows and contrasting fabrics make this comfortable chair even more inviting. The collection of antique toys and birdhouses adds a rustic charm to this relaxing corner.

Details of Design

How do we create a specific country style? What colors and fabrics do we choose? What about furnishings and accessories? As a country-style compendium, the chapters of this book offer information on all this and more, but before turning our attention to the various facets of country style, there are basic principles of good design that apply to any decorating scheme.

First and foremost, you'll want to give thought to what purpose each space in your house or apartment will serve. With the kitchen and bathroom this seems obvious, but perhaps a corner of the kitchen will perform double duty as a small home office space with a desk for the computer or paying bills. The same may be said of the dining room or possibly even a bedroom. The trend today is toward multifunctional rooms, given the increased number of people working at home and the amount of electronics that seem to have become a part of our daily lives. Fortunately the television, VCR, and stereo equipment can reside quite nicely in the large cupboards associated with a country decor. And having such high-tech gadgetry doesn't mean you're not living simply; it means you're simply living with modern-day conveniences that can be blended into a historical or nostalgic background to provide creature comforts such as good music or an evening spent watching an entertaining movie.

After deciding what practical purposes your rooms will serve, you'll want to give thought to the mood they'll set or the ambiance you wish to create. Fortunately, country decorating allows for flexibility, and patterns, textiles, furnishings, antiques, and collectibles of diverse ethnic origin or period design can be mixed nicely to create a warm, unpretentious, and welcoming setting.

Despite the fact that country style allows for a free hand in decorating, you'll still want to keep room proportion and balance in mind. This can be accomplished by using furnishings of relatively similar size, or by selecting pieces that are appropriate to the space in which they reside. Likewise, a room will be balanced when it's outfitted in such a way that furnishings, collections, and accessories are evenly distributed throughout the room and not grouped or bunched together, which would leave noticeable sparse areas or blank spots. Comfort and convenience are naturally the most important features of your room design, but you want the room as a whole to be aesthetically pleasing.

Any country setting will have one or more focal points that draw the eye, create interest, and give your room personality. The focus can be on an architectural feature such as a handsome fireplace, a furniture grouping, a display of collectibles or artwork, or even a single piece of folk art. Feature your personal favorites, whether they include a collection of stoneware displayed on built-in shelves in the family room, a grouping of chintz-covered easy chairs in the living room, or an antique iron bedstead in the guest room.

Finally, when it comes to selecting the background for any given room, color is a key element since spaces are generally decorated around a singular color or group of colors. Generally, color can be thought of in terms of primary, secondary, and tertiary hues. The primary colors are red, yellow, and blue, and from these three basics the secondary colors of orange, green, and violet are derived. The tertiary colors are then made by mixing a primary and secondary color; the results include red-violet, red-orange, yellow-orange, yellow-green, blue-green, and blue-violet. Adding white, black, or gray to any of the above opens up a world of color options of tints and shades. For example, pastels are popular tints used in country decorating, while navy blue is an all-time favorite country color shade.

A room's color palette usually falls into one of three categories: a complementary, analogous, or monochromatic scheme. A complementary color scheme uses colors directly opposite each other on the color wheel, such as red and green. This type of scheme is characterized by a bold use of color that can infuse a room with a lively spirit. In contrast, a more tempered use of color can be achieved using an analogous color scheme, which makes use of hues in close proximity to each other on the color wheel. A monochromatic color scheme is planned around a single color.

Last but far from least, many a wonderful country room has been designed by relying on neutrals such as white or beige to set the perfect backdrop for notable furniture pieces, folk art, and collections. Also keep in mind that several companies today are producing paints in old-fashioned colors reminiscent of the milk paints used long ago, such as mustard, bayberry green, cranberry, buff, or smoky blue. These colors are not only striking on walls and woodwork but in many instances are also ideal for reproduction furniture.

Take into consideration the natural lighting a room receives and the size of the room when choosing colors. Light colors or tints will make a small space appear larger, while deeper shades will make a large room more cozy and intimate. "Cool" colors such as blue and green can make for a restful, relaxing room; "warm" hues such as red or yellow are energizing and make a room appear bright and cheerful.

Pattern runs a close second to color in determining the overall character or ambiance of a country-inspired room. Pattern can help contribute a more traditional air, for example, with the flame stitching associated with a Colonial decor, or a casual, even playful mood, as with checkered patterns. Through pattern a country decor becomes visually pleasing, and the opportunities to include pattern in any given room go far beyond fabrics. For example, wall coverings and rugs can have strong impact in this regard, as can artwork or a display of treasured antiques and collectibles. No matter where your preference lies—whether it be stripes, florals, prints, or plaids—keep in mind that pattern can also be used to tie a room together. To achieve the best possible results, a blend of patterns will really make your room stand out. For example, combine a small-scale floral pattern on the walls with a larger floral pattern on upholstery and drapery for visual impact.

Texture is another important factor in planning your country home. Do you want rough plaster walls that imply old-world charm, a wood-beamed ceiling for a rustic look, or smooth painted walls that serve as a quieter backdrop for furnishings and decorative accessories? Texture is also a consideration in selecting carpeting or rugs, upholstery fabrics, window treatments, and accessories. Texture adds depth to a room and imparts a sense of the traditional or the decidedly casual to a decorating scheme. For the country home, rugged fabrics or other textures and collectibles such as baskets immediately come to mind.

These concepts can serve as a foundation for your country decorating, but it's your own personal interpretation of country that gives your home a truly signature look. For some, country decorating calls to mind the Colonial hearth and home, while others envision the quintessential American farmhouse or the cozy English cottage. Regardless, *The Country Home* is the perfect idea book to help you create the country rooms you long to live in. Comfort is paramount, and each facet of country style offers an abundance of opportunities for designing inviting, livable rooms that convey ease and the renewed sense of spirit that comes from a return to our roots.

Welcome to *The Country Home*.

Above: This lovely bedroom takes its cue from the Victorian era, with its passion for nature and love of collections. Embroidered flowers on the pillows echo the real blooms on the nightstand, while the antique hat boxes and family pictures recall days gone by.

Chapter One

Colonial Roots

One of the earliest American country decorating styles, referred to as Colonial, holds a proud place in many hearts and modern-day country homes. Not surprisingly, it is a country look with strong ties to tradition—time-honored furniture designs and decorative accessories that have endured for well over two hundred years.

With a long and distinguished history that can be traced back to the early part of the eighteenth century, the

Colonial interpretation of country style developed as the American colonists, settled into their various trades and businesses, lavished greater attention on their homes. From small timber-framed or saltbox dwellings to larger brick or Georgian-style mansions, the colonists furnished and decorated their homes with appealing colors, comfort, and sophisticated ease.

The predominant furniture styles during the Colonial era were Queen Anne and Chippendale, which had strong ties to

Above: Color and texture are a hallmark of Colonial country style. A muted red paneled wall and doors contribute an authentic decorative touch in this dining area while the bricked hearth, complete with beehive oven, clearly recalls the past. Windsor chairs are gathered around the table, and note, too, how old-time kitchen items enhance the Colonial setting. Opposite: This under-the-eaves bedroom speaks of sophisticated comfort and country charm. Colonial furnishings such as the upholstered wing chairs and tall case clock add instant style, and decorative touches such as the portrait above the dresser and floral scatter rugs show that notable details can have a big impact.

England. The Queen Anne style, in vogue from the 1720s through the 1750s, is noted for graceful proportions and a signature cabriole (having a soft S curve) leg found on chairs and tables. While the more formal or high-style Queen Anne furnishings were handcrafted in the important cabinetry shops located in Newport, Baltimore, New York, Philadelphia, Charleston, and other growing cities, rural artisans produced their own, often simplified versions of the Queen Anne style. Formal and more costly pieces such as chairs, drop-leaf dining tables, tea tables, high chests, and card tables were often fashioned from imported mahogany and featured intricate shell carvings on larger pieces. In contrast, the furnishings turned out by country craftsmen were made from readily available hardwoods such as cherry, oak, and maple and were more basic

in design, but their construction methods (mortise-and-tenon) were often every bit as skilled and accomplished as those of the master craftsmen. Country pieces were often painted for a unified look, especially if a combination of woods was used in their construction, and rush seats rather than fine upholstery were found on most country Queen Anne side chairs. The upholstered wing chair, an all-time country favorite, was most likely covered in woolens or a homespun fabric in the rural Colonial home, rather than expensive fabric imported from abroad.

Close in design but somewhat more ornamental than the Queen Anne style, Chippendale furnishings were popular from the 1750s through the 1790s. Rural craftsmen, however, often continued to produce furnishings based on these designs through the early 1800s. The more formal furniture pieces were handcrafted with scrollwork, carved Rococo shells, rosettes, and decorative fretwork. The delicate cabriole chair or table leg with a slipper or pad foot found on the earlier Queen Anne–style furniture became more masculine and sported a ball-and-claw foot in the Chippendale design.

Popular furniture pieces turned out in the Chippendale style included camelback sofas, upholstered open armchairs, large chest-on-chests, case clocks, candle stands, tea tables, high chests with bonnet tops, serpentine-front chests of drawers, and Pembroke tables. Once again the country craftsmen, more concerned with utility than ornamentation, created furnishings inspired by the Chippendale designs or a combination of two or more styles.

Other furniture designs in fashion during the Colonial era, especially in rural areas, were the slat-back chair and the Windsor chair. Each design was interpreted differently according to geographic location, so numerous variations of each were produced, for example, there were low-back, comb-back,

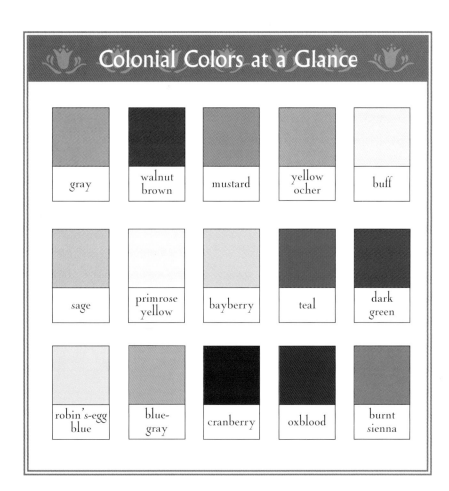

Colonial Colors at a Glance

gray	walnut brown	mustard	yellow ocher	buff
sage	primrose yellow	bayberry	teal	dark green
robin's-egg blue	blue-gray	cranberry	oxblood	burnt sienna

and fan-back Windsor chairs. Typically made of local woods such as cherry, walnut, pine, and maple, these early chairs were often painted black or deep shades of red or green to camouflage the fact that several woods were used to construct a single piece. These country chairs, as well as other painted furniture pieces, were often treated with pigments created from natural elements such as clay, berries, or other vegetable matter. Different shades of green were achieved by making use of the patina that developed on brass or copper. Linseed oil, skim milk, and water usually formed the base in making furniture paints, which is why you'll often hear references to "old milk paint" finishes when examining antique pieces. And simply painting a piece of furniture was

often not enough; if time allowed, many country craftsmen embellished a lot or a little with decorative graining or swirl designs made with combs, feathers, sponges, or even crinkled paper.

During the Colonial era, houses ranged from the simpler dwelling with painted plaster walls to the larger, more formal home that either had wood-paneled walls with architectural embellishments or walls with a wooden chair rail running around the perimeter of the best room or rooms. During the later part of the Colonial era, imported wallpapers from France with popular scenic designs were found in the homes of the well-to-do. And the colors that made their way into many a Colonial home were lovely, rich, and spirited. Oxblood,

Above left: Beautiful wide-plank flooring, a half-paneled wall, and striking architectural details on the fireplace wall combine to create the perfect Colonial setting. Colors that clearly recall the past have been chosen for the paint that adorns the door, moldings, and wood paneling. Select furnishings and artwork complete this simple yet lovely country-style setting.

Above right: Colonial roots are apparent everywhere in this bedroom complete with an antique desk, rush-seat chair, four-poster bed, and vintage trunk. Wood-paneled walls and a brick hearth with a handsome wood mantel add architectural detail, while select accessories, such as candlesticks and stoneware, enhance the Colonial country flavor.

The ultimate symbol of warmth and welcome, the hearth was the focal point of the Colonial home for practical as well as aesthetic reasons. Warmth and light were the paramount purposes, but a family gathered together around the fireplace, perhaps reading or doing needle-work, was an image depicted in paintings and described in many a printed page. The Colonial hearth became more elaborate during the mid- to late 1700s with the addi-tion of handsome mantels or over-mantels, often faux-painted to look like marble. In the majority of homes, however, the mantel

burnt sienna, yellow ocher, robin's-egg blue, bayberry, and dark green were just a few of the favorite colors used to beautify fireplace walls, paneled walls, doors, and trim.

and paneled wall surrounding the fireplace were painted one of the colors mentioned previously or a deep walnut brown.

Plank wood flooring was used in the Colonial home but was often covered with paint or a floorcloth; in wealthy homes expensive Oriental carpets were featured in the "best" room. Handmade braided and rag rugs were common in simpler homes where scrap materials—those that could no longer be utilized for clothing or linens—were put to use to make functional, colorful, and dec-orative throw rugs.

Above: Blue and white, long a favorite country color combination, is especially lovely in this Colonial sitting room. The half-paneled fireplace wall, mantel, expanse of bookshelves, and window shutters have been painted a winning shade of blue that here becomes a focal point. An inviting wing chair is positioned close to the hearth, while a small tavern table and Windsor chairs sit atop a handsome Oriental rug. Select treasures throughout add a very personal touch.

Windows during the Colonial era were treated to shutters or simple homespun curtains tied to the side. More elaborate festoons were used in formal settings, and while these were fashioned from costly imported materials, more typical households used muslin or other homey fabrics to serve as window dressings. Checkered or striped patterns were common, not only at windows but also for the bed curtains that helped provide warmth on tall, four-poster canopy beds.

Decorative accessories in the Colonial home were a clue to the family's wealth. Those households that could afford it often purchased fabric from abroad as well as Oriental porcelain, sterling silver flatware, English china, and numerous other items. In the majority of homes, however, the built-in corner cupboard held locally made pewter rather than a collection of good china, and dishware was more likely pottery or hand-crafted woodenware. In regard to special items, with the Colonial-era penchant for drinking tea most families could lay claim to a precious few imported teacups, which were not only highly prized but considered a wonderful extravagance.

While many of the eighteenth-century Colonial homes were formal in appearance, today's take on Colonial style is far more casual. And it's definite-

ly not a "period" look, unless you're creating a historic house museum. Rather, the Colonial interpretation of country style borrows key elements from the past to fashion rooms with a historic look but an abundance of comfort and relaxed appeal.

Above: An inviting four-poster canopy bed is dressed with a checkered fabric and a simple white spread. Now purely decorative, rather than a necessity as in days gone by, the canopy bed is quintessential Colonial country style. Note, too, the mustard-colored paint that has been used on the bedroom door and surrounding trimwork. A peek across the hall reveals a handsome oil portrait above the hearth.

Above: This casual country entryway sports a hard-working tile floor in earth tones that complement the vaulted ceiling and woodwork throughout. The loft railing provides the perfect spot for displaying country quilts, and an old-fashioned metal chandelier answers the need for lighting. Furnishings such as the lift-top bench, and accessories such as the baskets and hooked rug, add an element of Colonial spirit. An antique baker's cupboard serves as a focal point and enhances the country spirit.

The Colonial Entryway

The front hall or entryway of your home offers that all-important first impression of your personal style and your country decor. The front hall also needs to serve as a functional space for dealing with coats, boots, and rain gear. Thus, you want it to be both practical and inviting. With this in mind, flooring is an important consideration, given the fact that the vestibule calls for something durable yet appropriate to your Colonial country decorating scheme.

Marble and granite are two very strong, attractive options when it comes to flooring, but they should be reserved for the formal or high-style country home. For a more casual look, slate or ceramic tile are excellent choices, though a wood floor can be treated to withstand the hard use an entryway receives. Slate has a very natural look and proves ideal in an entry because it is less prone to becoming slippery than other hard flooring options. Another advantage is that the muted colors typically found in slate blend subtly with virtually any color scheme.

In contrast, unglazed ceramic tiles (with a matte finish to prevent slipping) can be used in the entry to create an exceptional rather than an understated flooring treatment. For example, consider designing a ceramic tile floor with a checkered pattern, or perhaps a decorative floral or geometric border. There are unlimited options available with a Colonial country theme in mind.

For those smitten by the timeless beauty of wood, a polished hardwood floor in the entry adds warmth and marked country style. For something a bit more bold, a wood floor can be painted to create a checkered or diamond design, or the floor can be stenciled with a country-style folk art motif. Be sure to seek information or manufacturer recommendations regarding floor care and the use of protective sealants.

Walls in the Colonial-inspired country foyer can be painted, papered, or treated to a decorative embellishment such as a chair rail or paneled wainscot. Save the rich wood paneling for a large, formal entry and consider instead an attractive play of colors to infuse this space with country ambiance. Colors that hark back to Colonial days, such as cream, mustard, blue-gray, or muted green, are ideal. Walls can be simply painted or paint can be combined with a wallpaper border or stenciled motif. Your choice of color will naturally be influenced by personal taste, the size of the entry, and the level of natural and artificial lighting it receives. Keep in mind that lighter hues are ideal in a small space while a large front hall can be made more intimate with deep shades.

Wallpaper patterns with a strong link to the Colonial past include scenic designs, toile de Jouy, large florals, the tree of life motif, and checkered prints. Naturally, small patterns are better suited to smaller spaces. Wallpaper was really only affordable for the well-to-do during the Colonial period, so it's associated with very traditional or high-style interiors. The general population made do with stenciled designs or the work of traveling artists, who would paint a scenic design on an interior wall in exchange for food and lodging.

Furnishings and decorative accessories for the front hall will be determined by the size of the space. Perhaps you have the perfect spot for a tall case clock, or a long wall ideally suited to an antique settee with a rush seat. For a more formal entry, a wing chair or two with a tea table or candle stand may be called for. In a more relaxed entry, Windsor chairs, painted ladder-back chairs, or even a painted bench may be more to your liking. Once your furnishings are in place, turn your attention to decorative accessories for lighting and visual appeal. For lighting, consider a simple hanging fixture with a glass globe or a reproduction iron chandelier with curved arms. Wall sconces, too, are a won-

derful addition to the entry; place them so as to get enough light not only for practical purposes but to show off accessories such as a collection of baskets, an arrangement of dried flowers, a pinecone wreath, a vintage oil portrait or two, or a grouping of pewter candlesticks.

Above: *This entryway may be small on space but it's definitely big on style. Rugged plank flooring and the green painted staircase immediately recall Colonial roots. With the addition of a rush-seated chair, a Colonial-style wall sconce, and a primitive lighting fixture, this welcoming vestibule is made complete.*

The Colonial Living Room and Dining Room

Moving beyond the entryway, the living room and dining room in the Colonial country home can take on the look of an old-fashioned keeping room or hall by mixing period-style furnishings with a neutral background so that furniture and accessories take center stage. To create a more historical look, keep in mind the traditional colors used in the Colonial home and paint walls a soft buff or cream, then finish woodwork, a fireplace mantel, or a fireplace surround with a bolder color such as oxblood or bayberry. In this way color becomes a focal point that blends with fabrics and textures in the living or dining room.

In a more subdued setting, walls painted in neutral tones such as white, gray, or beige can serve as an elegant background for handsome antique or reproduction furnishings and favorite accessories. You can let color make itself known via the upholstery, draperies, artwork, and collectibles on display. A stenciled frieze near the ceiling can always be added to create a soft and decorative effect that plays on the colors in furnishings.

Wallpaper is another option in decorating the walls of the living room and/or dining room. To achieve a casual look, a checkered design or floral pattern will do nicely. Toile, stripes, and scenic patterns are generally considered more formal but even these can be "relaxed" by blending just the right furnishings and other decorative patterns in the room.

Above: Furnishings take center stage in this Colonial-inspired living room where white walls provide the perfect backdrop. A scenic toile pattern on matching wing chairs goes quite nicely with a playful and spirited check on the sofa and twin ottomans. A lovely Oriental rug pulls the seating arrangement together, proving once again that patterns can be combined with beautiful results. *Opposite*: Combining color, pattern, and texture has resulted in an eye-catching arrangement. A classical table resides against an aged brick wall and provides the ideal spot for a colorful ginger-jar lamp. The antique doll carriage fits neatly below and an old wooden candle box makes the perfect addition on the wall. The floral patterned camelback sofa sports a warm throw for curling up, and the entire setting is one of cozy Colonial comfort.

The Elements of a High-Style Colonial Country Look

* Paneled or wallpapered walls (scenic, floral, and toile)
* Period furniture designs in mahogany
* Fabrics such as damask, chintz, and tapestry
* Oriental or Aubusson rugs
* Draperies made of brocatelle, chintz, and velvet
* Antiques and collectibles such as silver, china, brass, and crystal

The Elements of a Casual Colonial Country Style

* Painted walls
* Country renditions of furniture styles in cherry, maple, and oak or with painted finishes
* Homespun fabrics
* Hooked, braided, or rag rugs
* Curtains (sill-length rather than draperies)
* Antiques and collectibles such as redware pottery, woodenware, baskets, pewter, quilts, and folk art portraits

The wide plank flooring used throughout the Colonial house may suit today's country-style homeowner just fine, or you may aspire to something different. Both plank and hardwood flooring can be dressed with braided, rag, or hooked rugs for added color, texture, and pattern, or a more traditional Oriental rug can be called into use. Even those homes with wall-to-wall carpeting can be "countrified" by layering vintage or reproduction rugs, or rugs handcrafted by talented artisans, atop the carpet.

When it comes to windows, a simple treatment works best in the country home with Colonial spirit. Tab curtains, curtains hung and then tied back to the side, or decorative valances are all in keeping with this country style. If a more elaborate window dressing is desired, patterned fabric can be coordinated with upholstery or a damask can be used to fashion draperies or festoons. Then again, if your windows afford both a natural scenic view and privacy, the best window treatment may be no treatment at all.

Furnishings in the living room and dining room should be comfortable, such as a camelback sofa and wing chairs. The dining room table should be large enough to accommodate family and friends. For a traditional look the ever-popular flame-stitch pattern (with a multicolored flamelike design) is ideal on a sofa and chairs. A scenic tapestry is another option, but furnishings can also take on a relaxed or playful spirit if dressed in checks, stripes (such as ticking), or plaids. Brocades and damask, on the other hand, are elegant fabrics that will convey a high-style look, but they too are available in such a wide range of colors that you'll want to consider these options as well.

Other furnishings to consider for the more public spaces of the country home include a tall chest-on-chest, which can be put to use in either room. Perfect for storage, this large case piece contributes a notable dash of Colonial ambiance when in a Queen Anne or Chippendale design. Dining room chairs and side chairs used in the living room can be elegant period pieces or simpler Windsor or ladder-back chairs with rush seats. For casual country appeal, juxtapose a Queen Anne side chair with an indigo blue-and-white-checkered fabric on the seat or at the window.

Other pieces at home in the living room might include a country rendition of the tea table, a candle stand, a settee, a slant-top desk, a low chest of drawers, and upholstered open armchairs. Good choices for the dining room include a drop-leaf, gate-leg, or trestle table. And don't forget the corner cupboard: regardless of whether it's built-in or freestanding, a lovely corner cupboard has long served to put cherished or everyday items on display. At home in either the living room or dining room (or both), the corner cupboard can be painted to match trim work on walls or to provide a color accent.

Practical and decorative accessories in the living and dining rooms include artificial lighting sources such as table lamps, wall sconces, and overhead fixtures. A combination of general and task lighting is preferable and can be achieved in a number of ways. Metal and pottery table lamps with fabric shades and metal wall sconces, perhaps with a mirror back to reflect light (based on historic designs), are all in keeping with a Colonial theme. And we mustn't forget candlelight. Metal or pottery candlesticks will do nicely, and there's nothing that adds ambiance on a cold winter evening like the soft glow of candlelight used as a comforting and decorative effect.

Above: While this handsome case clock most certainly steals center stage, a glimpse through the doorway reveals a primitive free-standing cupboard that becomes a picture-perfect spot for favorite collectibles. Wide plank floors, sage-green paint, and a curved-arm iron chandelier create the perfect backdrop for these and other Colonial furnishings, such as the small tavern table and the Windsor chair in the foreground.

Above: This high-style traditional bedroom features a striking four-poster bed with lavish detailing. An equally beautiful spread, in neutral colors, complements the bed nicely. A rush-seated chair, slant-top desk, and simple bedside table complete the setting, while the room itself is made cozy and inviting via a wallpaper border and an Oriental rug.

Consider scented candles—perhaps bayberry—to enhance country sights with country scents.

Since country decorating derives much of its appeal from the utilitarian yet often whimsical household items of the past, surround yourself with your favorite objects or collections. With a Colonial country decorating theme in mind, baskets, pewter, redware pottery, Oriental porcelain, needlepoint samplers, and folk art portraits are just a few ideas for the living room and dining room.

The Colonial Bedroom

When we think of the Colonial-inspired country bedroom, a large four-poster bed immediately comes to mind. Regardless of whether the bed is canopied or not, it certainly serves as the focal point of any country bedroom. Dress it up with bed curtains or allow the handsome simplicity of the wooden posts to stand on their own.

The trim in the country bedroom can be painted in the old shades that say "Colonial" so well, while walls can be soothing in a pale cream or off-white. Even using a Colonial color to paint entire walls can have a comforting effect when you choose a soft gray-green or gray-blue. A stenciled design can always be added for heightened interest. For those who prefer paper over paint, a floral, stripe, or toile pattern can be especially nice in the bedroom and can be coordinated with fabrics, curtains, or the bed dressing for a high-style coordinated look.

Comfort underfoot is especially nice in the bedroom, so lavish a wood floor with area rugs. Braided, rag, or needlepoint rugs contribute a casual air while an Oriental rug imparts formality. Remember, too, that carpeting can be layered with small rugs for a heightened decorative effect.

Controlling natural lighting in the bedroom is an important consideration, so window dressings should be practical as well as decorative. Fussy tassels and fringe won't do in the Colonial bedroom unless you desire a formal look. Think instead of lined tab curtains, rod-pocket draperies that have simple but elegant rods with decorative finials, a combination valance and drapes, or a decorative swag. Fabric shades can be used as needed with any of the above; also, shutters add a nice touch in the bedroom, where they contribute subtle architectural flair.

Furnishings and decorative accessories in the Colonial bedroom naturally include the bed, and as mentioned previously, the four-poster canopy bed is the epitome of a high-style country look. You can dress this bed with layers of flowing fabric for traditional appeal or scale back and use a half-canopy approach with decorative fabric just at the head of the

Above: Casual Colonial country style is the decorating theme in this bedroom sporting a low-post bed with a colorful quilt. A primitive half-moon table resides at the foot of the bed, as does a small but handy trunk. An antique desk is the perfect spot for paperwork and small collectibles. Note, too, how a neutral backdrop brings out the deep green shade used at the window and echoed in the patterned area rug.

Redware Pottery

* This was the first pottery made in the United States, beginning in the seventeenth century.

* Redware colors range from dark red to brown to a light, almost orange shade.

* Redware was shaped by hand and allowed to dry; the glaze was applied by brushing, hand-dipping, or pouring, and the pottery was then fired in the kiln.

* Most redware was made in the Northeast, in Pennsylvania, Virginia, Ohio, Illinois, New York, and New Jersey.

* The slip-glaze applied to redware was made from ground clay, water, and lead, and ideally made the pottery more durable.

* Slip-glazes were frequently colored, so antique redware can feature folk art designs (swirls, flowers, or wavy lines) in black, brown, green, or orange.

* Redware was made until the 1850s, when stoneware and yellowware proved more popular.

* Decorated redware is quite costly, but collectors can still find plain pieces that are reasonably priced.

bed. For a more relaxed setting, eliminate the bed curtains altogether and let the beauty of the bed speak for itself. Other bedding options include a low-post bed, a cannonball bed, or even a handsome sleigh bed.

For storage in the bedroom a large chest-on-chest or high-chest can be used in tandem with a smaller four-drawer chest. A candle stand or tea table can make the perfect bedside table, and an antique or reproduction blanket chest can store bed linens at the foot of the bed. Don't forget to create a spot to relax: a comfy wing chair or two are perfect for reading or quiet conversation in the privacy of the bedroom.

Personalize your Colonial-style bedroom with favorite paintings, family photos, collectibles, perhaps some colorful bandboxes to store mementos, and warm, inviting bed linens. A fine handcrafted or antique quilt, a crewelwork spread, or a cheerful striped comforter invite curling up in bed with a good book. Scented candles and a fresh bouquet of flowers will make the bedroom that much more inviting.

The Colonial Kitchen and Bathroom

The kitchen and bathroom are known for the wear and tear to which they are subjected, so they need to be highly functional with durable surfaces. That doesn't mean, however, they can't be stylish and convey strong country appeal. On the contrary, Colonial spirit can take center stage in the kitchen and bath by calling upon historical colors, familiar patterns, and timeless textures.

Opposite: This warm and inviting kitchen conveys the essence of Colonial country style. A Colonial color palette and serious attention to detail—from the dried herbs and basket hanging from a wood beam to kitchenware on display—clearly recall the past. Slat-back chairs with rush seats are gathered about an antique table and colorful rag rugs serve to define specific spaces. All in all, this is the perfect spot to linger over tea and special treats.

Walls can create the perfect background when painted in authentic colors or when a neutral shade is used and accented with a bolder trim—perhaps an off-white with bayberry trim in the kitchen and a spirited robin's-egg blue in the bath. Several manufacturers are making paints available in old-time colors such as those featured in the historic buildings at Colonial Williamsburg in Virginia. Visit any quality paint store for a better idea of exactly what's available. To embellish painted walls you can always add a stenciled design or opt for some architectural flair with a handsome wood chair rail or plate rail, which can double as a display shelf for collectibles.

Wallpaper can be used in the country kitchen or bath provided it has a scrubbable surface. Again, check selections carefully to make sure that the paper you choose is appropriate to rooms subject to heat, steam, and moisture. Keep in mind that large florals, scenic patterns, and toile were Colonial favorites used in the very best rooms, and will undoubtedly give the kitchen or bath a high-style look.

Flooring in both the kitchen and bath is subject to heavy traffic, spills, and damp spots, so longevity and convenience are important considerations. Ceramic tile, resilient flooring, and wood flooring are the most popular options and each can be used to achieve a Colonial country look. Ceramic tile and inlaid vinyl flooring or solid vinyl tiles come in myriad colors and patterns, making it easy to match your color scheme. Geometric motifs, checkered patterns, and a decorative tile border are just a few possibilities at home in a Colonial-inspired kitchen or bath. A more rustic look can be achieved with quarry or terra-cotta tiles.

If you have a wood floor or are considering installing a wood floor in either the kitchen or the bathroom, you can make it really stand out by adding a stencil design or painting the floor with a checkerboard or diamond pattern. You can also give the floor a soft color wash and follow that up with a protective clear finish. For an aged look simply let wide plank boards develop the warm patina that comes with time.

Kitchen cupboards and countertops require a good deal of space to provide adequate storage and work areas for cooking and baking. You can almost consider them furnishings. In the Colonial-style kitchen, painted cabinets are ideal and can become a focal point of your decorating scheme. Regardless of whether you select an old-fashioned blue, green, red, or some other favorite hue, painted cupboards can be left that way or decorated with a stencil design. Simple wooden knobs are fine in the kitchen, but brass pulls will dress your cupboards and drawers up just a bit. If the warmth of natural wood is the look you desire, cherry, maple, or pine cabinetry can be used to imbue the kitchen with a casual country air. Keep architectural embellishment to a minimum unless your goal is a more formal look.

Kitchen counters can be functional and still say "country style." Wooden butcher block immediately comes to mind, but tiles afford you the opportunity to play with color and design. For example, use hand-painted tiles with floral or folk art motifs, or create patterns all your own with two or more colors of tiles. In addition, plastic laminates or solid plastics are sold in a rainbow of colors, so don't overlook this possibility when figuring your budget and your heart's desire in regard to surface space.

To enhance the Colonial country spirit in your kitchen, add a scrubbed-top worktable that doubles as a center island or a painted step-back cupboard for displaying dishware or pottery. Keep your window treatments simple by using linen, muslin, or cotton curtains in a floral or checkered pattern or even a simple cream or off-white. For lighting, an iron chandelier and simple sconces can create atmosphere, while hidden-from-view recessed lighting can provide much-needed task lighting at the stove and countertop areas. Collectibles on display will add the perfect finishing touch. Fill an antique or reproduction cupboard with redware pottery and hang baskets or dried flowers from a plate rail or wood-beamed ceiling. Put a casual bouquet of wildflowers on the kitchen table or counter.

In the bathroom, modern fixtures such as the tub, sink, and toilet can be played down by incorporating Colonial country touches that recall the spirit of the age. Playful checkered bath towels, a colorful braided rug, and old-fashioned wall sconces will hint at country style. For something a bit more dramatic a vintage or reproduction cupboard, commode, or small chest of drawers can be fitted with a sink and the necessary plumbing for a unique vanity. Use tiny baskets to keep soaps at hand and larger baskets for face cloths and towels. Place an antique or reproduction wood-framed mirror above the sink or add some high-style elegance with a gilt-framed mirror. As with any other room in the house, the goal is to make it convenient and comfortable—make it Colonial country.

Above: This glorious bath is infused with Colonial country spirit thanks to the notable chest of drawers that doubles as a vanity and the wood tub surround that blends beautifully with the wood-beamed ceiling. A delicate stenciled design dresses the bathroom walls, sconces have been added for lighting, and a needlepoint rug contributes a splash of color. Select artwork and collectibles, a simple window treatment, and a framed mirror complete this relaxing setting.

Chapter Two

French Ambiance

An overwhelming favorite from abroad, French country style is characterized by a palette inspired by the vibrant landscape of southern France and the gracious furnishings developed from a rural lifestyle. The earth of the region provides the clays that are transformed into beautiful French pottery, and for centuries artisans have created the striking Provençal fabrics synonymous with French country style. The colors, furnishings, fabrics, and sundry collectibles of the countryside bring French ambiance into homes all over the world.

Country style took center stage in the 1970s, and it was just a matter of time before we became enamored with other cultural takes on a relaxed and casual way of designing a home. By the 1980s French country style was making its mark in America, and its popularity has remained steadfast. And no wonder: it's a decorating style that developed over centuries to answer the need for practicality, acquiring an earthy—and elegant—look along the way. Generation after generation, the cottages, farmhouses, and even the grand châteaux in rural France were outfitted with family

Above: With a beautiful and scenic backdrop, dining alfresco is one of the many pleasures of a French country lifestyle. A rugged table and casual wicker chairs invite lingering over a tempting lunch or dinner. Colorful patterned fabric is ideal for placemats and a table runner, and fresh fruit, fine wine, and a touch of candlelight make for a most relaxed and enjoyable setting. Opposite: A handsome brass bed becomes the center of attention in a simple bedroom with subtle blue walls and a rugged chest of drawers. Layering printed fabrics creates a beautiful bed dressing, while comfort items close at hand—books, fresh water, and a bouquet of sunflowers—imbue the room with French country spirit.

furnishings handed down through the years, select pieces crafted to meet specific needs, and patterns and textures that made living spaces as appealing and inviting as the outdoors.

The color palette of the French country style has roots in the lavender and wheat fields of Provence, the sunflowers and poppies that bloom across the southern French countryside, and the stunning blue of a cloudless sky and the yellow of an intense sun. These colors blend brilliantly with the rustic, natural textures that find their way into the French country home, but they are perhaps most familiar in the cotton print fabrics long produced in France and used for upholstery, pillows, curtains, and other decorative items.

French Textiles

History tells us that printed cottons were imported from India to France as early as the seventeenth century. They proved to be so popular and in such demand that French textile firms attempted their own production of the coveted cloth. It wasn't long before this new cottage industry made inroads on the sales of established firms making silks and woolens, and as a result King Louis XIV banned manufacture of the colorful fabrics as well as the sale of imports from India. During the 1680s, however, weavers in both Avignon and Marseilles were able to continue small-scale production of the Provençal cloth, since those areas were not then subject to French law. In the 1750s the ban was finally lifted, and the manufacture of block-printed cottons flourished

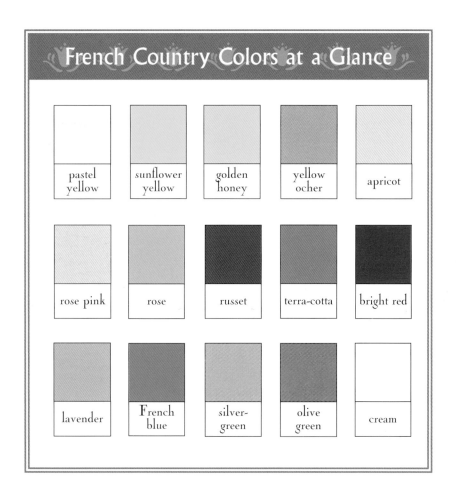

French Country Colors at a Glance

pastel yellow	sunflower yellow	golden honey	yellow ocher	apricot
rose pink	rose	russet	terra-cotta	bright red
lavender	French blue	silver-green	olive green	cream

Above: A lovely settee is dressed in a red and white toile de Jouy that's the essence of French country style. Matching pillows casually provide added comfort, while a backboard has been fashioned to keep favorite books within easy reach.

across France, especially in the city of Tarascon on the Rhône River, where the world-renowned Souleiado firm was established in the latter part of the eighteenth century.

The Souleiado firm, although known by various other names until the 1930s, has produced printed cotton fabrics continuously for more than two hundred years. While hand-blocking was the typical means of creating prints through the 1800s, the Industrial Revolution eventually ushered in more mechanized means of producing the cloth. Also, the vegetable dyes used to color fabric were replaced by synthetic dyes in the 1940s, but keeping pace with science and technology has not altered the beauty of the fabric, nor has it altered the age-old patterns and old-world colors that make these fabrics so spectacular. Designs, in fact, are often taken from the original pearwood blocks that have been preserved over the years.

French Provençal cottons, a hallmark of French country style, are typically adorned with small paisley or geometric designs as well as large or petite floral and fruit motifs. Over the years the various designs have been influenced by stylistic periods, but those mentioned above are favorites in the French country home. Colors, too, have changed from time to time, but the signature colors of Provence—bright blues, yellows, reds, greens, and lavender—continue to dominate and no doubt will for years to come.

Also used in the French country-style home are toile de Jouy printed cotton fabrics. Toiles de Jouy feature a white or an off-white background with a monochromatic pictorial scene. Popular colors have long been violet, red, and blue. The toile de Jouy that depicts peasant and landscape scenes is more in keeping with a French country decor than the classical motifs produced, which are a favorite in more formal settings.

Above: Sunny yellow walls happily coexist with the vibrant printed fabric that serves as an eye-catching table dressing, evoking French ambiance. Patterns are mixed with wonderful results by adding an oval-back armchair and delicate floral draperies for a truly signature touch.

lines, and carved, often symbolic designs. French country furniture is also made of natural materials such as wicker or sturdy wrought iron.

French Furniture

As with the various other interpretations of country, the furniture associated with French country style evolved from period designs over hundreds of years. The peasant lifestyle called for furniture that was, above all, functional. Rural artisans adapted traditional designs to suit needs based on a simple way of life. As far back as the 1400s furniture was crafted virtually without embellishments, but by the 1700s a distinctive style developed

The Oberkampf factory near Versailles was producing toiles de Jouy in the late eighteenth century and became well noted for their popular fabrics. Today there are any number of textile firms in France that continue the tradition. Toiles are especially popular for a more high-style or formal look, particularly when fabrics for upholstery and curtains are coordinated.

What would these old-world fabrics be without furnishings for prominent display? French country furniture, however, is much more than a sofa and an easy chair covered in a French Provençal print; it includes warm woods, curved

throughout rural France as craftsmen borrowed from the decorative forms of Louis XV–style furniture. The Louis XV period, synonymous with Rococo style, saw furniture crafted with graceful, curved lines and subtle or magnificent carvings based on motifs from nature. These attributes were carried over to the more modest furnishings crafted by and for country folks, and while many pieces were made of walnut, other local woods were used as well. For example, antique French country furniture can be found in cherry, chestnut, pearwood, olivewood, and mulberry.

The quintessential French country furniture piece is the armoire. In days past it was an important part of a bride's dowry and served to store the assortment of linens lovingly prepared by hand to set up a new household. Antique armoires from the Rococo period were often created with carved symbols of

Above: Simplicity is striking in this French country–style bedroom where an iron and brass bed sports a French Provençal cotton spread. A small but very decorative painted cabinet serves as a bedside stand, and a wireware sconce is positioned on the wall. A framed mirror placed above the bed is visually pleasing.

Above left: A lovely floral wallpaper plays up the color in a time-worn painted chest and an upholstered side chair with subtle curves. Clothing and hats on a peg rail become objets d'art, as does the mirror propped up on the chest. French country style is achieved by combining nature-inspired color, pattern, and texture.

Above right: An earthy hexagonal tile floor is juxtaposed with a decorative privacy screen and an easy chair upholstered in a French country–style signature color— red. This appealing corner invites relaxation and brings a touch of the outdoors inside in typical old-world fashion.

love and prosperity such as hearts, turtledoves, and sheaves of wheat. The armoire naturally held a place of pride in the Provençal home and was passed down from one generation to the next.

Other French country–style furnishings include rush-seat slat-back chairs (the slats are typically curved rather than straight), settees, dining tables, buffets, hall tables, chests of drawers, and numerous signature items such as the *panetière,* used in the kitchen for storing bread. Carved designs, which were often determined by regional tastes, and curved legs characterize the majority of pieces. Exceptions include the more rustic, utilitarian items crafted for humble households; these pieces have more in the way of moldings than carved designs. Finally, there were the simplest, most purely functional pieces, which were unadorned and only painted for decoration.

Decorative accessories and antiques associated with the French country style have long included detailed ironwork (on everything from doors and windows to furniture), hand-molded pottery, baskets, wire objects, handblown

Left: A rugged wood-beamed ceiling and tile floor play host to a striking armoire that holds a cachet of glassware. Beautiful paneled doors exhibit the graceful curved lines often found in French furnishings and this exceptional piece, actually built into the wall, has been painted in mellow hues that only grow more lovely with age.

glass, colorful tilework found throughout the French country home, ceramic or enamelware kitchen containers, and artistic enamelware wall-hung racks used in the kitchen for everything from cooking utensils to hand towels. Not surprisingly, many such objets d'art are kitchen-related and have strong ties to the celebratory manner in which meals are prepared and consumed in France.

The French Foyer

Creating a French country–style decor in today's home does not mean starting over from scratch. You can blend strong elements of this appealing style with what you already have in place. The result will be comfortable country rooms that combine graciousness with French flair. For example, if space allows, in the front hall or entry you can add a large French banquette or settee, which typically seats three people. This particular piece of furniture resembles a French country–style armchair in that it has a rush seat and curved slats across the back, and its length suits it to a foyer or even a living room, where it is usually situated near the fireplace. If space is at a

Right: By allowing the colors found in nature free rein, this French country–style foyer is the very essence of European ambiance. A cool, tile floor and white walls allow select furnishings—a rush-seat chair and small chest—to take center stage. To the right of the entryway a copper lavabo (French wall-hung containers used to hold water for hand washing) and basin filled with a dried bouquet add a subtle but elegant old-world touch.

filled with lavender, a wallscape of straw hats, or a tabletop arrangement of French pottery. Functional rather than fashionable is the key here; the beauty of simple objects imparts old-world style and appeal.

The French Living Room and Dining Room

The French country living room and dining room follow suit in that natural materials, print fabrics, and rugged rural textures take center stage. Color leads the way in determining fabrics and accessories. For walls, rough plaster can be color-washed, and even if you don't have plaster walls, modern-day wallboard or plasterboard walls can be painted in the same fashion—you just achieve the color without the textured surface. Keep in mind that the lines between indoors and out tend to blur in French country style, which takes its colors from nature. Your living room and dining room walls provide a subtle background for furnishings and accessories. Soft earth shades, the cool color of the sea, and floral hues are the colors to draw from. And don't forget the ceiling: in a great many rural French homes ceilings have dark wooden beams with white plaster filling in the gaps.

Floors in a French country living room or dining room are often paved with terra-cotta tiles, but ceramic tiles can also be used. Available in assorted sizes and shapes such as squares, rectangles, and hexagons, tile has long been the preferred choice for flooring in the south of France, where it stays cool dur-

premium, other furnishings at home in the foyer include a hall table and a chair or two—perhaps outfitted with cotton print cushions in vibrant French hues.

The entry can also convey French country appeal by incorporating natural elements such as a tile floor or a wood-beamed ceiling. Walls in the French country home are usually a cool, whitewashed plaster, which serves as the ideal backdrop for fabrics and homespun textures. With this in mind, paint walls white or a soft version of a French country color. Walls should have a subtle look—like the almost faded patina that develops over time. Add an iron chandelier or wall sconces for lighting; decorative touches can include a basket

Above: This spacious foyer imparts French country style by combining a rush-seat banquette (settee) with pale, color-washed walls and a blue and white pictorial tile insert that becomes an instant focal point. A small tree in a beautiful jardinière adds a decorative touch to this welcoming entry and enhances the "natural" French flavor.

ing the summer months and is easy to keep up. Add to that the fact that clay is an abundant natural resource in Provence and it's no wonder that tile can be found throughout French country homes.

Terra-cotta tiles feature a burnished red coloring, and their earthy hue and slightly uneven texture add considerably to the French country ambiance of the living room or dining room. A terra-cotta tile floor can be dressed up with an accent or area rug in cooler months, or a rug can be used simply to define space. Colorful rag rugs are ideal for a casual setting, while an Oriental rug will contribute a sophisticated contrast. Also consider resilient flooring, which offers an array of handsome decorative options at a fraction of the cost of tile. Determine your budget for flooring; you may want to consider a quality vinyl tile with the look of terra-cotta tiles.

Furniture in the French country living room or dining room is casual—not at all formal. Pieces crafted from walnut or fruit woods predominate, and fabrics are generally the cotton prints long associated with French country style. For relaxed ease in the living room, a comfortable sofa and an easy chair or two can be upholstered in a French Provençal print, a toile de Jouy pattern, or an easy-care fabric in a solid color that is accented with pillows designed from a traditional print fabric.

Chairs and side chairs with curved slats and woven rush seats are perfect for providing extra seating in the living room, where they can be outfitted with colorful cushions. Wicker furnishings are also a welcome addition to the living room, where their natural texture will blend beautifully with the French country theme. Assorted small tables, whether made of wood or created with an iron base (perhaps with a glass or marble top), are both functional and stylish.

Above: This sun-drenched corner of a French country dining room demonstrates the simple beauty of lace panels used as a window treatment. By adding such items as a rush-seat chair, a small chest, select artwork, and a bouquet of fresh flowers, the spirit of the style is celebrated.

An armoire in the French country living room? Absolutely. Actually, the armoire can be used in any room since it's not only ideal for storage but can also serve as an entertainment center or, if fitted with shelves, a display center. Naturally a valuable antique should not be significantly altered or its value will decrease considerably.

As for dining room furnishings, simple yet elegant is the key. A long rectangular table or a rustic round table can be accompanied by slat-back chairs, wicker chairs, or chairs sporting a wheat-sheaf design on the back. Even a wonderful settee or banquette can be pulled up to a rectangular table. For storage in the dining room, a buffet is the perfect addition. French country craftsmen fashioned low case pieces with two cupboard doors that open to reveal shelving for dishware, table linens, and cutlery. Buffets can be quite simple and plain with little in the way of embellishment except for moldings, or they can be more decorative with carved designs.

Window treatments in the French country living room and dining room are light and airy. Lace has long been a favorite in this type of country decor, used alone or as an undercurtain. A Provençal print can be used to design curtains or draperies. Look to iron curtain rods or simple wooden rods when choosing the hardware for window dressings, and don't forget a decorative finial for the perfect finishing touch. Naturally if either room has a private view or perhaps French doors leading out to a secluded patio for alfresco dining, you can leave them bare and enjoy the scenery. To control natural light, matchstick or bamboo blinds offer the rugged accent that exemplifies a country French decor.

Decorative accessories and collectibles might include an iron chandelier in the dining room and iron- or pottery-base table lamps in the living room. Fabric shades can always be coordinated with upholstery, pillows, or curtains

Above: The armoire, at home in any room of the French country–style house, is ideal in the living room for rounding up books and cherished treasures. This beautiful example, with paneled and glass doors, has been painted to create a decorative effect. Placed against a white plaster wall it becomes a stunning focal point.

for a dressy look. There are numerous choices when it comes to lighting, so keep in mind that metal, wicker, and pottery fixtures are all in keeping with a French country theme.

Other decorative touches may include favorite pottery pieces displayed atop the mantel or a grouping of colorful plates hung on a wall. Colored glass bottles and candlesticks blend nicely with the color palette of a French country setting. And don't forget that baskets—filled with lavender, sunflowers, fruits, or vegetables—can be put to use in myriad ways, and their notable texture and earthy colors express strong country style. Other items might include a large wicker trunk used as a wonderful coffee table or two or three trunks of various sizes stacked to serve as a side table.

When it comes to baskets, don't overlook wire pieces, which can also make a bold decorative statement. Wirework was practiced by many European artisans during the nineteenth and early twentieth centuries, and wire baskets are available in a seemingly infinite variety of shapes and sizes that prove ideal for decorating today. While antique examples can be costly depending upon rarity or design, current reproductions can bring European ambiance to any room in the home. You may just want to fill a large wire basket with fresh vegetables and use that as a centerpiece on the dining room table. Then again, you may want to

cover the table with a Provençal quilt and let an antique soup tureen become the center display.

Above: Sunflower-yellow walls, patterned, tailored draperies, and a decorative parquet floor play host to a wonderful collection of French furnishings in this semi-formal country setting. A rush-seat settee is positioned in front of the window and laden with comfortable pillows. Cane-back, cushioned chairs surround a beautiful table with elegant curves and an embellished apron. An antique lighting fixture, nature-inspired prints, and a bouquet of what else—sunflowers—make this dining room a French country–style treat.

The Elements of French Country Style

❀ Vibrant cotton print fabrics

❀ Rush-seat chairs, armoires, and rustic furnishings with curved lines and carved motifs

❀ Lace curtains

❀ Color-washed walls, terra-cotta floor tiles, and wrought-iron hardware and decorative accessories

❀ Collectibles such as baskets, French pottery, colorful glass bottles, vintage enamelware, wire items, and copper cookware

❀ Decorative accessories such as flowers, dried herbs, and centerpieces arranged from fresh fruit and vegetables

If your living room or dining room is graced with a fireplace, a tile fireplace surround is certainly in keeping with the French country spirit. Tile, after all, is used liberally throughout Provençal homes and expresses the essence of this spirited country style. Whether you opt for tiles in a single striking color, hand-decorated tiles, or a decorative pattern created from two or more colors of tile, you can create a highly personal design for your fireplace that puts a one-of-a-kind mark on your home.

The artwork you select for living room or dining room walls may be landscape scenes or perhaps Impressionist prints. Then again, it may be the modern artwork you love or the unusual oil painting you discovered at the flea market. French country style is not tied to period designs, so allow yourself the pleasure of enjoying the artwork that "speaks" to you and becomes a welcome addition to your home.

Above: Selective restraint is a hallmark of French country style when it comes to collectibles and decorative accessories. Something as simple as candlelight, fresh flowers, or potted bulbs can speak volumes about your penchant for a country lifestyle. Opposite: Special paint techniques can be used to create any number of decorative effects in a French-inspired country home. This fireplace wall has a marbled appearance that blends sensually with rustic pottery, baskets, and a warm, wood floor. The nature-inspired printed fabric on the easy chair echoes the earth tones and provides choice seating beside the hearth.

The French Bedroom

French country decor does not rely on an overabundance of "things" for its strong appeal. Rather, select items are casually integrated over time with what is needed to make a comfortable home. With this in mind, a French country bedroom is almost spare when compared to a bedroom decorated in the English cottage style, for example. Low, wood-beamed ceilings and color-washed plaster walls are typical, and tile or wooden floors are perhaps outfitted with rag rugs or sisal matting for added comfort underfoot. That is not to say that all French bedrooms are created equal: there are those with lovely wallpapers, carpets, and a bit more in the way of accessories and decorative touches. It's simply a matter of personal taste.

Furnishings in the bedroom include the focal point—the bed—as well as a wardrobe for clothing and a bedside table along with a chair or two. The bedstead most often found in the French country home is painted in a pale hue and has a scalloped headboard with posts. Low posts are featured on the simple footboard. Other styles of beds at home in this interpretation of country include a headboard with rounded corners, delicate floral carvings, and, once again, low posts at the foot of the bed. Metal beds, too, are perfect in such a setting—either brass or iron, but simple in design.

Windows in the bedroom are dressed in airy lace panels or cotton print curtains. Bamboo shades or shutters can also be used to filter light. Outfit the bed with a quilted bedcover made from a Provençal cotton print, or use a pretty crocheted bedcover and lace-edged pillowcases. Keep creature comforts close at hand on a bedside table—a metal or pottery lamp for reading, a favorite book or two, a clock, and perhaps a vase filled with lavender or wildflowers.

Opposite: Outfitting the French country bedroom to fulfill basic needs affords simple elegance. Here, an old iron bed displaying soft curves and aged green paint is dressed with a colorful cotton spread and lace-edged pillows. A lace panel filters light at the window and a rustic painted bench becomes a perfect bedside table for books and a miniature bouquet of flowers. Above: Blue-gray walls and looped-back pastel draperies make a pretty backdrop for a beautiful iron bed with a plump comforter and an abundance of pillows. The hardwood floor is softened with a patterned area rug and a rugged bedside table keeps favorite objects close at hand.

The French Kitchen

The French country kitchen is truly the center of the Provençal home. Kitchens in Provence tend to be large, reflecting the importance of cooking in France. Such kitchens feature a rustic, wood-beamed ceiling and rough plaster walls color-washed in a favorite tint. Many kitchens also feature extensive tile-

Above: French ambiance is achieved in this kitchen by calling upon a generous use of ceramic tiles to create a one-of-a-kind backsplash. A variety of kitchenware close at hand, such as baskets, pottery, and an assortment of canisters, further enhances this interpretation of country style.

work—not only terra-cotta floor tiles but also ceramic tiles on the walls. Half-tiled walls and tile used for a backsplash or as an insert behind the stove are common. Tile is also used on many kitchen tabletops. While white tiles with a blue floral or geometric design have long been popular in the countryside, so too are vividly colored tiles arranged in checkered or diamond patterns. And hand-painted tiles can add a distinct decorative touch to the French country kitchen. In creating a French country ambiance in today's home, you may want to consider resilient flooring with the look of tiles if your budget suggests it, and select a specific area in the kitchen—say, the countertop or the back-splash—on which to use decorative tiles for a stylish accent.

Furnishings in the French country kitchen often include a series of free-standing cupboards rather than built-ins, though sometimes a combination of both is used. Wooden dressers, a hutch, and an armoire all provide storage space. Metal baker's racks are also widely used and provide abundant space for dishware, kitchen staples, and cookware. Little is hidden from view in the French country kitchen: hutches and cupboards have glass doors and shelves edged in decorative lace or a French cotton print. The kitchen table is often large and rectangular, and is accompanied by an assortment of chairs made of wood with rush seats, or metal bistro chairs.

Other furnishings that have long been a part of the French country kitchen were designed to meet specific needs. For example, a wall-hung *panetière* for storing bread was de rigueur in Provençal kitchens during the nineteenth century. Small in comparison to other French furnishings, the *panetière* was unusually ornate and elaborately embellished with carved spindles and various regional motifs such as flowers and wheat sheaves. A small door situated in the front of the boxlike container allowed bread to be placed inside or taken out, and the evenly spaced spindles next to the door and on the sides of the box allowed air to circulate around the freshly baked bread. This small, handcrafted item was often the masterpiece of the kitchen, a testament to the skill and talent of the Provençal artisan.

Small wooden *étagères* were also found in the French kitchen and these, too, were hung on the walls to hold an assortment of kitchenware such as dishes, glasses, and cutlery. *Étagères* could be plain and simple or fairly ornate. Some examples were treated with a decorative cotton print fabric backing.

Kitchenware on display and close at hand in the French country kitchen creates a decorative effect all its own. Gleaming copper pots and pans are hung within easy reach of the stove, pottery bowls or wireware baskets full of fresh fruits and vegetables sit atop the table or a handy cupboard, and vintage or modern-day enamelware containers and cookware are distributed throughout

Above: Making sure that everything is within a cook's reach is an important stylistic consideration in a French country kitchen. Here, blue and white tiles serve as an eye-catching countertop and backsplash, while the cookware suspended from an overhead rack is practical as well as decorative. A vintage scale and fresh flowers complete this picture-perfect setting.

to hold an array of staples and brew coffee. Some French country kitchens still have (and use) a striking enamelware stove made during the early 1900s.

Perhaps because the French kitchen is such a beehive of activity, a closer look at the everyday items long used there is called for. A Provençal print fabric and white pottery dishes make a striking setting for the kitchen table. Faience has been made in a variety of colors for centuries, and another type of French pottery called Quimper is popular worldwide and is named after the French town in which it's made. Quimper has been produced since the 1600s, and avid fans of this pottery decorated with peasant figures, nature designs, and folk art motifs seek out vintage examples as well as the dishware that is being made today.

A surprisingly large number of wire objects were handcrafted during the late 1800s and early 1900s for use in the kitchen. Serious collectors and Francophiles are always on the lookout for wire baskets made to hold eggs, fruit, pastries, bread, and lettuce. There are also vintage wire kitchen utensils, racks for cooling cakes or cookies, wire-framed plates used to served fruit or pastries, trivets, wire glass carriers, and even wire wine racks. These old-fashioned wares were often embellished with intricate, lacy designs and curlicues, and a collection displayed in a hutch or on a wall provides a strong measure of old-world charm in the kitchen.

Vintage enamelware made in France and other European countries (often for the French market) came in a wide spectrum of colors and with various

Above: Color and select accessories imbue this kitchen with the spirit of French country style. A vibrant French-blue cupboard is ideal for storing dishware and a blue and white tablecloth dresses up the kitchen table. Touches of red—in the painted chair and the candlestick lampshade—reinforce the use of a French country color palette. Notice that the table sports a square wire basket ideal for storing condiments.

Opposite: Rugged textures, such as terra-cotta floor tiles, pine cabinetry, and a serenely handsome pine armoire, add instant French style to this kitchen. The spirit of the style is also found in the herbs drying on a wall-hung rack, the numerous kitchen items on display, and the lovely use of a printed cotton fabric on the chair cushions.

decorative designs. A variety of items was made for use in the kitchen, but collectors and those decorating in the French country style are especially taken with French coffee biggins. Coffeepots with removable midsections that hold wire mesh or cloth socks for filtering the popular brew, coffee biggins were made in a range of sizes. The great majority of them display decorative graphic designs ranging from floral motifs to geometric Art Deco patterns. Entire matching sets of enamel items were produced with the kitchen in mind, and,

today, old European enamelware (called graniteware in the United States) is eagerly sought by interior designers, collectors, and of course those decorating a French country home.

To create your own French country kitchen, keep in mind the colors, textures, and kitchen-related items that convey the spirit of the style so well. You can add decorative touches to create the ambiance of an old-world setting without forsaking modern-day conveniences. A single furnishing such as an armoire or baker's rack can be added to your kitchen to introduce instant style. Add some pottery, wire baskets, copper cookware, or enamelware and you've added French flavor. Incorporate a French cotton print in the form of curtains or a decorative tablecloth and you've got a bit of Provence at your fingertips. Use your imagination, express your personal style, and make it convenient, comfortable, and above all welcoming.

The French Bathroom

The bathroom in the French country home is generally simple and functional. Old-fashioned fixtures remain in place as long as they are serviceable. White is the preferred color and as a result, the bath often reflects a late-nineteenth-century ambiance. A crisp tile floor, ceramic tiles on the walls, a claw-foot bathtub, and a large pedestal sink create stunning beauty. Accessorized with a gold- or bamboo-framed mirror, wall sconces with etched glass globes, handsome chrome hardware, a wicker hamper, and luxurious white towels, the bathroom becomes a testament to the beauty of simplicity. Add lace curtains and toiletries grouped in a rustic wall-hung cupboard.

For a more obvious or spirited French country style in the bath, use a cotton print for window and even shower curtains, and perhaps for a cushion on

Vintage European Enamelware

* Look for pieces made between the late 1800s and 1940.
* Popular graphic designs include floral motifs, birds, stripes, checkered patterns, and Art Deco designs.
* Items made for the kitchen include pots and pans, wall-hung utensil racks, saltboxes, matchboxes, towel holders, canister sets, coffeepots, coffee biggins, teapots, measuring pitchers, and utensils.
* Many items made for the French kitchen have French lettering, such as *allumettes* on matchboxes.
* Look for rare or unusual items. Those items with graphic designs tend to be cosly while other pieces are generally reasonably priced.

a side chair. You may opt for a wallpaper rather than tiles—perhaps something with a floral motif, a toile pattern, or a combination of ribbons and flowers in a geometric design. Add select artwork and fill an enamelware pitcher with lavender, poppies, or sunflowers. Then fill the tub (include a bath gel scented with lavender or verbena for a truly French touch), relax in the bath, and imagine yourself in your country house in Provence.

Left: Simple, functional, and beautiful—this is the French country–style bath. A dual pedestal sink combined with a claw-foot tub endows this room with turn-of-the-century charm. The rustic wood beam, vintage armchair, matching mirrors, and towels add distinctive, practical touches. *Above:* The abundance of natural clay found throughout the French countryside makes a tiled bath such as this a natural. The vintage-style tub and curved sink rest nicely against the crisp white tiles of the wall and floor. Note, too, the use of pattern in the floor for heightened visual interest.

Chapter Three

Rustic Adaptations

Of the numerous interpretations of country style, rustic adaptations are perhaps the most fanciful, the warmest, and the most organic. A style that is defined most certainly by furnishings, rustic also refers to a style of architecture and to home accessories that have close ties to favorite outdoor pastimes such as hunting, fishing, or travels that encompass the wilderness areas of the great outdoors. As one circa-1904 rustic furniture catalogue so eloquently put it, "Nature unadorned is most adorned of all."

What we have come to think of as rustic style actually has roots in the lavish European gardens of the eighteenth century. The well-to-do paid great attention to the details of their formal gardens. A particular, rough-hewn style of chairs, tables, settees, planters, and decorative arbors made from shrubs and trees developed out of a need to escape—if only for a short while—from the urbanization and crowds of people in growing cities and urban centers such as London and Paris.

Above: An appealing arrangement of family photos calls upon rustic elements to fashion one-of-a-kind picture frames. The large photo has been treated to a natural wicker frame for an outdoorsy look and smaller photos are arranged in whimsical little "houses" with an aged, painted finish. Red, a favorite rustic color, provides the perfect background. Opposite: "Rustic" is much more than an interpretation of an interior design style—it can also refer to architecture such as this homey log cabin. Plank walls and a vaulted ceiling embrace an eclectic blend of furnishings that includes a beautiful twig chair. Accessories such as the colorful throw rug, camp bedding, and personal mementoes complete the vacation cabin theme.

porches, and flower gardens. The Niagara Falls Rustique Manufacturing Company was producing such items as early as the 1840s, and the company was known for the wide variety of items for decorating offered in the fashionable "rustique" style.

As the Victorian era progressed, rustic style came to be associated with the great camps built in New York's Adirondack Mountains and other vacation areas of the Northeast. Large camps and summer houses were constructed of logs and then furnished with cedar, birch, maple, or oak chairs, settees, tables, beds, and cupboards crafted by local caretakers, mountain guides, and a small number of skilled artisans. Most furnishings were made not only to outfit the summer homes being built but to provide a means of income during the long winter months. Adirondack rustic furnishings are generally angular in shape, and many pieces sport artistic mosaic twig work or applied decorations crafted from birch bark.

Regional variations in rustic furnishings were found across the United States. Craftsmen used available local woods and other natural materials to develop furniture styles that are now associated with specific geographical areas or ethnic groups. For example, in the Appalachian Mountain region, willow, laurel, rhododendron, and hickory wood were used most often to construct furnishings. From the late 1800s through the Great Depression, artisans fashioned assorted furnishings for the tourist trade as well as resort hotels, and items made in Virginia and North Carolina tend to display more curves and a softer form than the rugged Adirondack furnishings.

Although the term *rustic* is traditionally associated with furniture crafted from indigenous trees, some furnishings incorporate steer horns and moose antlers. Found mainly in the American Southwest, these materials were used by

By the mid-1800s America was being introduced to picturesque gardens and landscaping, and neo-Gothic-style planters, window boxes, tête-à-têtes, and benches were being crafted of twisted roots and tree branches for parks, front

Above: The log walls and plank ceiling of this country-style bedroom are accompanied by furnishings—bunk beds, desk, and chair—fashioned from branches and twigs. A birch-bark lamp, framed prints featuring fish, a plaid carpet, and deep-toned throw pillows enhance the rustic air of this inviting retreat.

craftsmen to fashion tables, chairs, footstools, and lamps during the late 1800s and early 1900s. Other furnishings were made from juniper and pine, and turn-of-the-century cowboys are credited with making a great deal of the rustic furnishings that ended up in ranches and tourist destinations. In typical western fashion, many such items were upholstered with furs or leather.

Both the gypsies that roamed the southern regions of the United States and the Amish of the Appalachian Mountains also designed rustic furnishings that have come to be identified with each group. The gypsies worked with willow to create pole chairs, which are easily recognized by their straight arms and legs and looped backs. The Amish also worked with willow but their chairs and rockers typically feature a bentwood back, so called because the willow shoots were bent to the desired shape using steam.

Rustic Furniture

During the late nineteenth century the demand for rustic furnishings was so great that several companies located in Indiana were eventually formed to produce a variety of items for resort destinations, summer homes, and parks located all across the country. The Victorian penchant for "getting back to nature" via trips to mountain lodges, wilderness camps, summer cottages, and the rugged terrain of the western frontier gave rise to the large-scale production of what was once a cottage industry to serve the tourist trade. As a result, the Old Hickory Chair Company of Martinsville, Indiana, was founded in 1892 to meet the need for a wide assortment of rustic furnishings, and its goods were almost completely handcrafted of hickory wood. The company's product line included everything from the Andrew Jackson chair (named after "Old Hickory" himself) and couches to beds, dining room sets, and children's furniture.

Antique Rustic Furniture

❋ Most pieces found today were made between the late 1800s and 1950.

❋ Not only are rustic furnishings the hallmark of rustic style, but many pieces are today considered a form of folk art.

❋ While a manufacturer's label can be a clue to origin and even age, this does not necessarily elevate the value of a piece since so many beautiful items were handcrafted by unknown individuals.

❋ Chairs, tables, and planters are still fairly easy to find in the antiques market, but larger items such as settees, desks, dressers, and buffets are rare and therefore costly.

❋ Adirondack furniture made with intricate, mosaic twig work or birchbark veneer commands top dollar—some items can cost thousands.

❋ Inspect furniture carefully for rot or insect damage. Pieces may or may not have been treated for these.

❋ Be aware that many modern-day artisans have rekindled the craft and are turning out exceptional examples of rustic furniture for today's home.

Its chairs were crafted with woven strips of wood that served as sturdy chair seats and backs. A company catalogue from the early 1900s describes the furnishings as ideal for "country clubs, lodge rooms, summer camps, golf clubs, hotels, verandas, lawns, bungalows, roof-gardens, and airdomes." Indeed, rustic furnishings could be used just about anywhere.

The Old Hickory Chair Company, which was making a great deal more than just chairs, changed its name to the Old Hickory Furniture Company in 1922 and actually remained in production until the 1960s. With the renewed interest in rustic furnishings and the awareness of rustic as a popular country decorating style, the Old Hickory Furniture Company came to life again in the 1980s and today continues the fine tradition of crafting everything from chairs, tables, bedroom furnishings, and entertainment centers to custom-made pieces from hickory saplings.

Other companies that were located in Indiana and are credited with turning out rustic furnishings include the Rustic Hickory Furniture Company, the Indiana Willow Products Company, the Jasper Hickory Furniture Company, the Indiana Hickory Furniture Company, and the Columbus Hickory Furniture Company. These firms were operating between the early 1900s and the 1950s,

Above: Even small details can have significant impact in rustic country style. By introducing just a single piece, such as a twig planter, a small log stool, or a birch bark ladder, a front porch or sun room acquires significant rustic flair.

but the most prolific period of rustic furniture production was from the turn of the century through the 1930s.

There were also smaller firms producing rustic furnishings in the Great Lakes region, one of which was the Rittenhouse Manufacturing Company of Cheboygan, Michigan, which supplied rustic cedar furnishings for summer homes throughout the northern Michigan area. The Rittenhouse Company was in operation from the late 1920s through the early 1950s, and according to one of their catalogues, their handcrafted furniture styles could be traced back to "designs from the Historic Indian Tribes of Michigan."

Many of the rustic furnishings produced by these companies were marked in some fashion, either with a metal tag, a paper label, or the manufacturer's name burned into the wood. Just as many, however, were unmarked, and since a great deal of vintage rustic furniture is making its way into today's antiques market, buyers should become familiar with the various types made and inspect pieces carefully for sound construction. Generally, chairs and small tables can be found easily, but larger items are rare and costly. Fortunately, there are beautiful handcrafted examples of rustic furniture being made today by talented and skilled artisans. Also, as mentioned previously, the Old Hickory Furniture Company is back in business (see Sources). The Adirondack Museum in Blue Mountain Lake, New York, is the site of a yearly antiques show held in September that features rustic furniture and all manner of decorative accessories as well as the works of contemporary craftsmen.

Far from being an uncivilized or uncultured furniture form because of its organic nature, rustic adaptations contains pieces that actually exhibit subtle period designs or tendencies. It has already been noted that early pieces designed for the garden displayed neo-Gothic characteristics. In addition, during the late 1800s, rustic furniture was in keeping with the Art Nouveau movement, in which the sinewy forms and curves of nature captured the attention of architects, designers, and the population in general. Rustic furnishings were also adopted by the proponents of the Arts and Crafts movement, who found honesty, simplicity, and beauty in the many objects fashioned from tree branches, twigs, burls, knots, saplings, and shrubs. With this in mind, the rustic approach to today's country decorating can coexist happily with furnishings and decorative accessories from the Victorian era and the Arts and Crafts period. A contemporary setting can also be infused with country charm by adding select pieces of rustic furniture or accessories.

The Rustic Entry

To create a rustic country home you don't need to live in a log cabin or a cedar-shake cottage by the lake, although both are architecturally synonymous with this country style. A high-rise apartment or suburban ranch house will do just fine, as either can take on the appeal of a relaxed vacation setting simply by bringing a touch of the outdoors inside. For example, a front hall or an entryway can immediately convey rustic spirit if you introduce a coat tree made of hickory, a rustic twig table for keys and a tabletop lamp, or a rustic willow or hickory chair. If space is limited, a wall-hung rack with pegs can serve as a spot for coats and hats.

Emphasize the rustic country spirit of the entryway by adding favorite photos, prints, or artwork in twig or birch-bark frames. A willow basket or two filled with dried flowers or pinecones will contribute to the effect. For lighting, your options are almost limitless; if you admire the metalwork of the Arts and Crafts movement, then by all means add a period ceiling light fixture.

Above: The inviting foyer of this log home extends a hearty welcome. Architectural embellishments, such as the rustic branch stair rail, serve to enhance the laid-back country spirit of this western retreat. Furnishings such as the twig table and a pair of rugged side chairs prove practical as well as playful and beckon visitors indoors.

If, on the other hand, a western look is your passion, you may want something a bit more bold such as a hanging fixture made out of antlers. Add a scatter rug or two—a floral needlepoint, a striped rag rug, or one with a geometric Native American pattern.

Part of the beauty of rustic style is that the furnishings and accessories blend beautifully into any color scheme. Bright colors, muted shades, pastels, and neutral colors all make an ideal backdrop for nature-inspired furnishings. Walls in the entryway or any other room in the house can simply be painted, or a bead-board paneling or wainscot can be added and then painted forest green or stained a honey pine for an outdoor look.

Above: *Painted furniture pieces are ideally suited to a rustic interpretation of country style. This eye-catching entryway showcases a green painted chimney cupboard, and accessories such as baskets, duck decoys, and a geometric-patterned rug convey a passion for the great outdoors.*

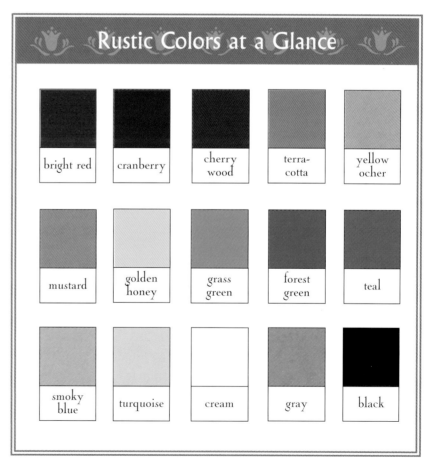

Rustic Colors at a Glance

bright red	cranberry	cherry wood	terra-cotta	yellow ocher
mustard	golden honey	grass green	forest green	teal
smoky blue	turquoise	cream	gray	black

The Rustic Living Room

Since rustic country style is so closely tied to the great outdoors and carefree, casual living, the living room should convey a hearty welcome and allow rustic furnishings to take center stage. Unless you're outfitting a vacation cabin, you'll most likely want to blend select rustic pieces with upholstered furnishings. A comfortable sofa and big easy chair (perhaps with a matching ottoman) can be dressed in easy-care fabrics such as denim, corduroy, hopsack, or striped cotton ticking. Such fabrics are available in a variety of rustic colors and can be accessorized with pillows made from Navaho blankets or rugs for western spirit, or with floral pillows for a lakeside cottage look. And speaking of florals, chintz is surprisingly beautiful in a rustic setting, in which the floral motifs of the glazed-cotton fabric complement the rugged appeal of twig, root, or willow furniture. Chintz fabric that has an aged look (often accomplished by soaking the fabric in tea) is especially lovely in a rustic decor, as are patterns with muted shades of green, gold, rose, pink, or teal. And if you happen to have log or plank wood walls, a cotton print fabric can add a much needed dose of color and pattern. For those who prefer a rustic style recalling the spirit of the Old West, leather furniture and animal prints will give the living room a frontier look.

Rustic country decorating is never contrived; add other furnishings and decorative accessories to suit the theme but express your personal interests and style. Combine a hickory chair or settee with wicker furnishings or favorite pieces of Mission oak inspired by the Arts and Crafts period. Lighting can take its cue from the Victorian age by incorporating antique or reproduction lamps such as a student's lamp or banker's lamp with a colored glass globe for tabletop use. Other possibilities might include wicker lamps (tabletop or floor

Above: The spirit of the Old West reigns supreme in this spacious log home. The mammoth stone hearth becomes a focal point that blends effortlessly with finished timber walls. Overstuffed furnishings, an assortment of comfy throw pillows, and striped scatter rugs create casual comfort. For lighting, a chandelier fashioned from antlers pays homage to the rustic theme.

lamps), metal lamps, pottery-based lamps with fabric shades, or lamps crafted from wood, antlers, or horns specifically for the rustic interior. All sorts of folk art lamps with fish, wildlife, and other motifs from nature are also being produced by talented artisans.

Since color is a matter of personal choice in a rustic country decor, hardwood, plank, or even carpeted flooring can be accessorized with scatter rugs or a larger area rug. Needlepoints, rag rugs, Navaho rugs, and even Oriental rugs (in your favorite colors, of course) can be added for warmth, pattern, and texture in the living room.

Other decorative accessories that are at home in the rustic-style living room include paintings or old prints in twig or birch-bark frames; souvenirs from hunting expeditions (such as taxidermy); outdoor equipment retired from use such as vintage fishing reels; old snowshoes; antique camp; lodge, or cottage signs; canoe oars; and pack baskets, as well as the myriad objects in miniature that were (and still are) handcrafted from wood for the tourist trade. Examples of these small folk art items include tiny canoes, carved animals, little log cabins, and furniture pieces. In log homes with massive wood beams and log trusses, some homeowners have even been known to hang an antique canoe from the rafters—now there's a rustic statement!

Above: The natural properties of wicker make it an ideal furnishing in a rustic country decor. Pine planking creates a rugged backdrop in this living room, which has an expanse of windows and a sliding glass door that beckon the outdoors inside. A casual, cushioned wicker chair with a diamond motif is joined by a simple footstool, a bouquet of dried flowers, a casual rag rug, and an example of taxidermy. Note, too, how the snowshoes propped against the deck convey the rustic spirit.

Opposite: Much more than a decorating style suited to vacation homes or summer camps, rustic style is also a favorite in year-round dwellings such as this one. An easy chair upholstered in an Indian print invites curling up in front of the hearth. Plank walls and flooring add instant warmth. Decorative accessories, such as the piece of architectural salvage atop the mantel, the basket used to store firewood, and the eye-catching model ship add signature touches that personalize and define this inviting space.

The Elements of Rustic Style

- Rustic furnishings

- Navaho prints on upholstery, pillows, and blankets

- Upholstery in stripes, plaids, leather, and even chintz

- Accessories such as taxidermy; decorative accessories made of metalwork, twigs, bark, willow, antlers, and horns

- Collectibles such as camp signs, rustic frames, hunting and fishing memorabilia, canoe oars, snowshoes, and rustic items made in miniature

Above: A rustic theme inspired by the Old West combines everything from an Indian print throw on the sofa and a geometric area rug to tables sporting wagon-wheel-style bases in this country living room. A pottery collection, a framed wagon train painting, and a metal and wood lamppost with an old-fashioned kerosene lamp impart frontier flair.

The Rustic Dining Room

The dining area in a rustic country home may well be an extension of other living spaces, since an open floor plan is popular among those who are building today's log homes. Then again, the dining area may be a room unto itself, off the kitchen or on an enclosed porch. Regardless, choose a color scheme that pleases you, then furnish and decorate to suit your needs and personal taste. Many of the dining room furnishings crafted by rustic furniture companies were made with guests in mind. Some vintage (and reproduction) round or square tables can extend to eight or twelve feet (2.4 or 3.6m). You can opt for an oak-top gate-leg or other drop-leaf table that will fit snugly against a wall. Benches or rustic side chairs can be pulled up to the table for seating and accessorized with colorful cushions for added comfort.

Other tables would be equally suitable in a rustic dining room. Consider a rugged picnic table with benches or a wicker table with an assortment of rustic or wicker chairs. Even a glass-top table with a wrought-iron base can be striking when surrounded by hickory chairs. Add a rustic buffet or serving table for storage space and accessorize with pottery dishes or plates with a woodlands theme. A display of dishes with a pattern of leaves or hand-painted animals can make an eye-catching arrangement on the wall. A birch-bark basket filled with flowers can make the perfect centerpiece, and candleholders made of silhouette-cut iron (perhaps of a deer, moose, or bear) can be a whimsical addition to the fireplace mantel. And speaking of fireplaces, even if your home doesn't have the river-stone fireplace associated with rustic dwellings, a rugged log or handsome gleaming wood mantel can still impart rustic style.

For lighting in the dining room, hang a chandelier or other fixture above the table—perhaps something that recalls the Victorian era (with a hand-painted

Above: Reminiscent of the great camps of the Adirondacks, this impressive dining room features a large, rectangular table constructed with logs and decorative twig work. Hickory chairs crafted with intricate designs provide seating for eight. The backdrop is decidedly simple, emphasizing the warmth of wood tones and the scenery beyond the windows. Select decorative touches atop the table—pottery, candlesticks, and a wooden bowl filled with fruit—create a picture-perfect table setting.

The Rustic Bedroom

or colored glass globe), an Arts and Crafts metalwork fixture, or a fanciful piece of modern ironwork. Wall sconces can provide additional general lighting especially if placed high on the wall, near the ceiling. Iron, pewter, or pottery candlesticks can be scattered about for a romantic ambiance.

The rustic bedroom of the old camp days has been made a bit more inviting and comfortable. Surround yourself with the colors you love and layer rugs underfoot for a truly soft touch. Naturally a rustic log or willow bed is appropriate to this particular country theme, but so too are other beds. Consider, for example, metal bedsteads painted in bright colors or a wooden headboard sporting pine tree or animal cutout designs. Painted metal beds in

Above left: This handsome dining room takes on a rustic air by adding a metal chandelier with silhouette cut-outs of woodland moose. Warm wood furnishings, a timbered ceiling, and a beautiful step-back cupboard filled with a collection of glassware and dishes make an ideal country decor.

Above right: Select pottery pieces and a serving tray with a delicate fern imprint that becomes wall art infuse this lovely setting with rural style. The patina of the time-worn tabletop is the ideal surface for trays with a similar nature-inspired motif and a handful of apples.

a rustic country bedroom should be basic and plain without ornate curlicues or designs—unless, of course, they contain nature or animal motifs. Many of the rustic beds being crafted today combine hand-forged iron with carved logs for truly spectacular headboards and footboards.

Vintage cottage-style furniture can also be mixed into a rustic country-style setting, so that antique bed you've had your eye on just might work beautifully. Cottage furniture was made during the second half of the nineteenth century for middle-class homes and vacation homes. Usually made of pine, these pieces were painted in pastel colors or brown and decorated with hand-painted floral motifs or stencil designs. Their casual spirit and decorative flowers and vines make them a natural in a rustic setting, especially when combined with a log chair or two.

Along with beds offered in twin or full sizes, other furnishings crafted by the rustic furniture manufacturers with the bedroom in mind include dressers, chests of drawers, vanity sets (including a small table and stool), luggage stands, mirrors, and table lamps. Throw in a chair or two—or even a rustic chaise longue—and you've got the ideal rustic retreat. And while today's bedroom may not be entirely decked out in log or hickory furniture, any of the above, whether an antique or modern creation, can turn the bedroom into an inviting sanctuary. For example, painted dressers or chests can be combined with a rustic bed, or a metal bed can be complemented by a rugged chest of drawers. Wicker or cottage furnishings can take on a rustic air by introducing appropriate decorative accessories, along with a rustic chair or desk. The possibilities are endless.

Rustic accessories at home in the bedroom might include old travel postcards casually tucked into a mirror or more formally grouped and framed.

Favorite prints can be arranged in an informal group on a bedroom wall—with twig, birch-bark, or carved wooden frames, of course. Have fresh wildflowers on hand in a pottery vase or in an old graniteware jug. Add a tabletop lamp for

Above: Perfect for a child's bedroom or a secluded vacation cabin, this single bed sports a sturdy headboard with a decorative decal and a Western spread. Navaho-patterned pillows add color and design while leaving no doubt that this interpretation of country was inspired by a passion for cowboys and a love of the Old West.

bedtime reading and make the bed cozy with coverings that are as inviting as they are practical. A warm comforter in a bold red or deep green can be accented with pillows made from Native American prints. A bright plaid throw or bedspread hints at a western theme. A floral spread or comforter can work surprisingly well—try using chintz curtains to match. The bedroom, after all, is a private place to escape to, and since rustic is a style for year-round

Opposite: The bedroom in this log home juxtaposes beautiful and sturdy log beds and a pair of hickory rockers with soft and delicate lace tab curtains at the window. Lace edging on the bed sheet plays nicely against the bold red and black checkered blanket used as a spread. Small touches, such as the Navaho blanket tossed across the back of a chair and the carved decoy on the trunk before the window, contribute country appeal. Above: A rustic tabletop vignette, at home in any room of the house, can be assembled with select elements of nature. By simply stacking smooth stones and adding family photos in handsome wood frames, an eye-catching still life achieves pleasing results.

homes—not just cottages, cabins, or lodges—you'll want to personalize the bedroom. The secret is to allow your imagination to be your guide.

The Rustic Kitchen and Bathroom

The kitchen and bathroom in a rustic country-style home can be as modern and efficient as needed for convenience and still convey a strong rustic feeling. Log or plank walls, a tongue-and-groove ceiling, or wooden posts and trusses will instantly create a rugged feel, but you can also create cabin-like appeal by whitewashing barn-board walls or adding bead-board paneling. A more subtle effect can be achieved by painting the background in a neutral shade and allowing a few well-chosen furnishings and accessories to impart rustic charm.

Kitchen cupboards can be a crisp white with iron pulls or knobs, or you can opt for the warmth of wood tones. Oak or pine cabinetry will lend the kitchen a woodlands atmosphere, but you should select plain cabinets without architectural embellishment—ornate moldings would be too formal and out of place in a rustic kitchen. Kitchen cupboards with the rustic look of bead-board are also fitting and can be painted or varnished to develop a mellow patina over time. Even Shaker-inspired cabinets with simple wooden pulls can be mixed with rustic furnishings and accessories for a back-to-nature look. Glass-front cabinetry with the appeal of an old cottage pantry cupboard can be a wonderful way to show off a homey mix of everyday pottery or dishware.

Furnishings in the kitchen naturally include a table and chairs. Accessorize a rustic table with a medley of chairs (rustic, wicker, or painted) for a casual, laid-back approach. Or how about a sawbuck picnic table with benches? If the kitchen is spacious enough you may want to consider adding a primitive painted cupboard for storage and display, or you may prefer to have a rustic

Above left: The kitchen in a rustic country home can be highly functional as well as decorative—there's no need to forsake modern conveniences. This kitchen calls upon natural elements to impart a handsome and rugged country style, inlcuding wood flooring accessorized with a rag rug, wood cabinetry, and ceiling beams.

Above right: Honey-color beadboard cabinetry in the kitchen blends beautifully with the massive logs used in this home's construction. Decorative elements such as the red area rug with a geometric motif, a hickory stool, and a crock filled with fresh flowers add rural charm.

step-back cupboard custom-made. Other ideas include rustic stools pulled up to the kitchen counter for snacks or a rustic desk placed in that perfect corner so that you have a spot for cookbooks or the home computer.

Accessorizing a rustic country kitchen should be fun. Scout auctions and antiques shows for old camp, lodge, and cottage signs that can decorate kitchen walls. Flea markets are still a good source for inexpensive pottery made from 1930 to the 1950s that will suit a rustic theme. More costly but beautiful are the pottery pieces associated with the Arts and Crafts period. Add cast-iron cookware or old graniteware and wooden items such as a large wooden bowl that can be filled with fruit. Place a rustic hanging light fixture or perhaps a light with a pierced-tin design of animals or trees above the kitchen table or the countertop area. An antique or a reproduction Victorian fixture that combines brass with a colored glass shade (green, blue, or white) can also suit the rustic kitchen.

Any bathroom can be given a dose of rustic charm by adding select furnishings and accessories. Bring in a hickory chair or table and add a willow basket or two for soaps, towels, or magazines. Above the sink or vanity, place a mirror that has a notable carved wood, twig, or birch-bark frame. Consider using iron wall sconces with colorful glass globes or whimsical plaid fabric shades. Throw an area rug that sports a geometric design atop a tile or wood floor, or add a floral needlepoint or rag rug for summer-cottage appeal. Simple cotton curtains in a muted shade or with a soft print will work well, and you can add wooden rods with black iron finials to enhance the rustic theme. Then light a scented candle (pine, of course), fill the tub, and relax in your cozy rustic environment.

A final thought: rustic adaptations are also ideally suited to decorating outdoors. Don't forget the front porch and the backyard deck. Adirondack chairs

are perfect in either spot for enjoying a lazy afternoon. A design that was patented in the early 1900s by an inventor in Westport, New York, the Adirondack chair has become synonymous with rustic style and perfect leisure, and fine handcrafted examples can be found in painted or natural wood finishes. Add a rustic table, fill a planter or flower box with blooms, pour a glass of iced tea, and leave the world behind. Now that's rustic country style!

Above: Here, rustic style has come full circle. What began over two hundred years ago as a decorative design in the garden still holds appeal and an abundance of natural charm. Simply put, a cushioned willow chair and chaise longue, accompanied by a rustic twig table, create the ideal outdoor retreat.

Chapter Four

Shaker Simplicity

The Shaker interpretation of country style has its roots in the religious beliefs of the United Society of Believers in Christ's Second Appearing—a religious sect commonly known as the Shakers. For more than two hundred years their timeless furniture designs have inspired a style of decorating based on the very same tenets that the Shakers had in mind when furnishing their communal homes: simplicity, utility, and craftsmanship.

Ann Lee (known as Mother Ann Lee) of Manchester, England, traveled to America in 1774, and within just a few short

years she and several followers who made the journey with her had established the first Shaker community in Watervliet, near Albany, New York. In an effort to inspire additional communities and see their fellowship grow, the Shakers traveled throughout the Northeast as well as to Ohio, Indiana, and Kentucky. Shaker communities were founded in New Hampshire, Maine, Connecticut, and the middle states, with the largest community located in New Lebanon, New York. This was the site of the main ministry of the Shaker sect, and in the 1860s the city name was changed to Mount Lebanon.

Above: Simplicity is the hallmark of Shaker country style. A ladder-back chair sits before a window featuring trim dressed in a deep red paint. A stoneware jug filled with flowers has been placed atop a small stool for a touch of natural beauty. *Opposite:* An unassuming entryway takes on subtle beauty by keeping furnishings and accessories to a minimum. White walls, painted doors and trim, and the simple good looks of a wood floor are all in keeping with Shaker style. A small bench holds a collection of tinware for visual appeal.

Shaker Furniture

The furniture crafted by the Shaker brethren was typically uniform, although slight variations have been found in the chairs created by different communities. Generally, however, similar pieces were made to outfit not only large dwellings but outbuildings and meetinghouses. Each piece of furniture was made without ornamentation and as straightforwardly as possible. Embellishing furnishings, in fact, was perceived as sinful since it took time that was better devoted to God.

The craftsmen and cabinetmakers at the various Shaker communities made a variety of furniture including side chairs, armchairs, rockers (usually reserved for the elderly), settees, tables, benches, large storage cupboards, desks, candle

Although Mother Ann Lee died in 1784, her work continued through the efforts of others, and the Shaker life principles of simplicity, purity, harmony, and order guided their daily lives as well as the handiwork they created for their large dwellings, which often accommodated several dozen believers of both sexes. Mother Ann Lee's words, "Hands to work, hearts to God," continued to inspire the Shakers for well over a hundred years after she was gone.

Above: *The spirit of a Shaker interior is achieved by placing a singular piece, such as this candle stand, against a wood-paneled wall. Through the doorway a low-post bed with a blue and white coverlet and a floor accessorized with needlepoint area rugs can be seen. Serenity reigns supreme with simple, basic furnishings.*

stands, blanket boxes, dry sinks, step stools, footstools, washstands, and beds, which were usually twin-size as chastity was an important part of their lifestyle and religious beliefs. These furnishings were constructed of pine, maple, cherry, chestnut, birch, or butternut and usually displayed exposed dovetail joints. Case pieces such as large storage cupboards for the kitchen were often built into walls, and drawers were labeled in an orderly fashion to identify their contents. Other furnishings featured narrow cupboard doors and simple wooden pegs used as pulls, and, as was often the case, a single piece of furniture could be built to serve more than one purpose. Many items were simply given a coat of varnish, while others were painted yellow, red, or green.

The chairs constructed by the Shakers early on were far different from the chairs they sold to the "outside world" during the late 1800s and the early 1900s. During the height of the Shaker movement—between 1800 and 1860, when membership increased from one thousand to six thousand brothers and sisters—their craftsmen fashioned ladder-back side chairs with three slats and armchairs with four slats, all of which curved at the top. Chairs were made in different sizes to accommodate specific individuals or for certain tasks. Early chairs featured pegged construction and seats made of cane, rush, splint, or tape. The tape seats used on early Shaker chairs were handwoven from wool and included a cloth lining filled with horsehair to lend additional strength to the seat. Regional variations can be found, for example, Shaker communities located in Massachusetts primarily made use of rush for seats while at Mount Lebanon cane seats were preferred.

The finials incorporated on Shaker chair posts also show small variations in earlier versions. In New York State the chairs were crafted with an acorn finial, while in the Shaker communities located in Maine chairs were topped with a ball-shaped finial. A flame-shaped finial was popular in Massachusetts, Connecticut, and New Hampshire.

Toward the end of the nineteenth century the Shakers began the commercial production of furnishings and assorted other goods, which they sold through catalogues and general stores located near their religious communities. Although they were mainly a self-sufficient group, these sales were intended to raise funds for those staples or household items they couldn't produce themselves. The chairs crafted during this period, roughly the 1870s through the 1930s, displayed glued rather than pegged slats and machine-made fabrics used as tape seats. A measure of hands-on work had to be sacrificed to meet

The Elements of Shaker Style

- Shaker furniture including chairs, rockers, benches, stools, cupboards, tables, desks, and candle stands
- Homespun fabrics in white, natural, stripes, or checks
- Rag or braided rugs
- Decorative accessories made of metal, wood, and stoneware
- Antiques and collectibles such as woodenware, stoneware, baskets, Shaker pantry boxes, Shaker brooms, and Shaker Seed Company boxes, posters, and prints

the demands of "outsiders" who were smitten with Shaker furnishings. Shaker chairs and rockers, in fact, received a great deal of notice after being given an award at the 1876 Philadelphia Centennial, where they were honored for their "Strength, Sprightliness, and Modest Beauty." Modest beauty indeed—even with the few shortcuts used in construction to fill the public's demand, Shaker chairs nevertheless maintained the simplicity and purity of form that have in many cases caused them to be considered works of art.

A Mount Lebanon catalogue published during the 1870s advertised a variety of chairs including slat-backs and web-backs (with tape backs as well as seats) and noted that chairs were available in eight different sizes—the smallest being a child's chair. The catalogue also pointed out that tape seats could be ordered in fourteen different colors, including three variations each of blue and green, gold, brown, black, drab, scarlet, orange, maroon, and pomegranate.

Along with chairs, rockers, stools, and benches the Shakers sold brooms, brushes, seeds, and oval pantry boxes that were available in assorted sizes with or without a colorful painted finish. And speaking of painted finishes, furniture and everyday objects were color-coded to a degree: yellow and red were used frequently, while blue was reserved for furniture in a meetinghouse and green signified furnishings and items used by members of the ministry.

Although Shaker goods were sold until the early 1930s, the membership within the religious sect dropped considerably and several communities closed. To date the only Shaker community still in existence is at Sabbathday Lake, Maine, where actual Shaker rooms serve as an apt background to

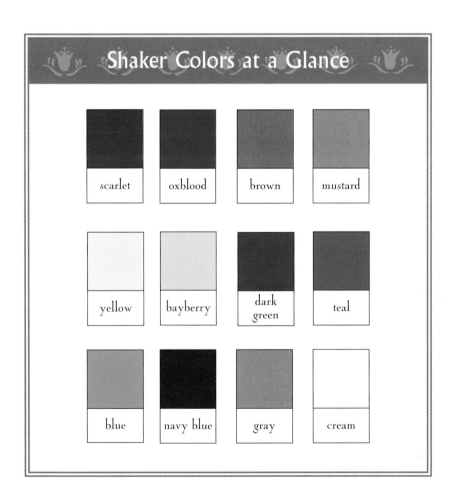

Shaker Colors at a Glance

scarlet	oxblood	brown	mustard
yellow	bayberry	dark green	teal
blue	navy blue	gray	cream

Above: Utility, simplicity, and fine craftsmanship were the qualities that determined the nineteenth-century Shaker interior. Then and now, the pleasing lines of a chair, such as this interpretation of a Windsor style, and the crisp design of a small Shaker stand, create striking, elegant beauty.

museum displays of handcrafted Shaker furnishings. Collectors and anyone else interested in exploring the history of these exceptional people and their furnishings may wish to visit the living history museums at Shaker Village of Pleasant Hill in Kentucky, Hancock Shaker Village in Massachusetts, or Canterbury Shaker Village in New Hampshire (see Sources).

The interior of the Shaker dwelling was outfitted simply; order, utility, and cleanliness were paramount. Wooden floors were left bare and walls were usually a neutral color such as off-white or cream with woodwork painted in deep shades of red, green, blue, or mustard. Aside from the minimalist furnishings, beautiful cupboards built into walls for storage, and what few personal belongings the Shakers had, one of the most notable features in almost any given room was the pegboard, which was used to hang household utensils, articles of clothing, and even chairs. It was placed around the perimeter of the room and consisted of a length of wood with evenly spaced pegs that were either painted or left natural. As far as accessories were concerned, textiles were made to provide only what was absolutely necessary such as clothing, bed linens, and simple homespun curtains used for privacy—not decoration.

Shaker simplicity as an interpretation of today's country decorating can be achieved by calling upon the elements of Shaker interior design and, of course, Shaker-style furnishings and accessories. While vintage Shaker furnishings and other handcrafted items can today command hundreds of dollars, there are excellent examples being created by modern-day artisans and a firm called Shaker Workshops, which has a mail-order service and a showroom located in Arlington, Massachusetts (see Sources). Keep in mind that Shaker

Above: This inviting kitchen calls upon several elements of Shaker design to give the room country spirit. Note how the plank wood floor is left bare for ease in cleaning and the white walls are accented with colored trim. A Shaker pegboard provides the ideal spot for keeping clothing and other items out of the way and yet well within reach. A handsome storage cabinet and secretary, Shaker in spirit, if not in design, nevertheless adds warmth and country style. Last but not least, a wood-burning stove provides all the comforts of home with a Shaker armchair drawn close to enjoy the warmth.

furniture, because of its simplicity and honest beauty, blends with period furnishings as well as other country pieces and can even be introduced into a contemporary setting with striking results.

The Shaker Entryway

The simplest and most obvious way to imbue the front hall or entryway with Shaker style is to hang a pegboard for coats and hats. To be a bit more obvious you may want to paint walls in a soft white or cream and treat trimwork to your favorite deep color—perhaps forest green or navy blue. A bare wooden floor in the entry isn't always practical, so an area rug such as a braided rag rug (even a needlepoint would look lovely) will help protect the floor. If room allows, add a ladder-back Shaker chair and side table, a candle stand, one of the many reproduction furnishings being crafted today such as a coat stand made with arched legs and a tripod base, a tape-seat settee, or even a beautiful case clock to enhance the Shaker look.

Add an overhead fixture or chandelier that conveys eighteenth- or nineteenth-century design, such as an iron fixture with curved arms or a handsome tin- or pewter-finished example. Pewter or tin wall sconces—electrified for convenience—will add Shaker country charm. For the perfect finishing touch add a woven splint basket filled with dried flowers. Remember, simplicity is the key; you don't want to overaccessorize and diminish the focus on the furnishings that are the hallmark of Shaker style.

Above: Soothing white walls, simple plank flooring, and a cozy, cushioned window seat for enjoying the view set the tone for this Shaker-inspired setting. By adding a homespun rag rug, fabric window shades, and a time-honored Shaker ladder-back chair, we see once again the timeless charm of streamlined serenity.

Opposite: Shaker simplicity is key to the beauty of this attractive vestibule. Cream-colored walls and a deep red trim are drawn from the Shaker color palette. Select furnishings, including a ladder-back armchair and a trunk for storage, add strong country appeal. The lighting, in the form of a metal chandelier and wall sconce, is perfectly in keeping with this scaled-back decorating scheme.

Above left: Traces of faded blue paint linger on the back door in this kitchen entryway. Wide plank flooring wears the patina typically acquired with age and walls are whitewashed for practicality. A painted table keeps a collection of kitchen jars handy while sundry household necessities are stored below. This simple Shaker-inspired setting quietly pays tribute to the past.

Above right: The essence of Shaker style is created here by painting doorway trim an old-fashioned shade called mustard. Less is more when it comes to furnishing this foyer, where a handsome case clock becomes the single focal point. The addition of a pleasing area rug contributes a restrained hint of color and design.

The Shaker Living Room and Dining Room

A Shaker-inspired living room or dining room can be modern-day comfortable and still impart serene Shaker style. While Shaker dwellings had little use for comfortable, upholstered furnishings, today's take on this attractive country style allows for a pleasing blend of inviting pieces and straightforward Shaker chairs, rockers, and tables. Neutral backgrounds or typical Shaker color schemes show furnishings to their best advantage, so give thought to the colors you choose for these two rooms. And while hard-

wood floors are very handsome in and of themselves, for convenience you may prefer carpeting. Select a shade that won't compete with furnishings for attention and focus. Not to worry—your goal is the essence of Shaker style, not necessarily a literal rendition.

The sofa and easy chair in the living room can be upholstered in handsome solid colors or a simple plaid or stripe, such as ticking. Limit pattern somewhat since simplicity is the goal. For additional seating you can mix Shaker chairs with other traditional pieces or contemporary furnishings. Reproduction Shaker chairs (or other forms of seating) with tape seats can actually be quite

colorful, and you can select from solid-colored fabrics or spirited checkered patterns that combine two distinct colors, such as blue and black.

For lighting in the living room use floor lamps and/or table lamps made with a pottery, wood, or metal base and linen shades. Table lamps created with a stoneware base are reminiscent of the blue decorated stoneware widely used

Above: Drawn from the subtle elegance of Shaker design, this dining room incorporates a hallmark wall treatment (white walls, colored trim) with carefully chosen furnishings and accessories. As a salute to Shaker style the owners have outfitted an antique table with ladder-back chairs and hung a simple metal chandelier. Other decorative elements, such as paintings, books, and flowers, are the essence of country spirit.

around the house during the nineteenth century and blend nicely in a Shaker-inspired decor. Lighting specialty stores and quality craft fairs featuring the works of skilled artisans and potters are excellent hunting grounds for suitable lamps and lighting fixtures.

Living room and dining room windows can be outfitted with simple tab curtains or tailored curtains of cotton muslin for strong country appeal. White or natural are ideal for a neutral color scheme; curtains can be embellished a bit with colored ribbon, embroidery, or a stenciled design to coordinate with upholstery fabrics. For a lighter touch, a fishtail swag or valance may be all that's called for. In contrast, a more traditional festoon and jabot will contribute a high-style polished look. Remember, too, that custom wood blinds are available in a variety of finishes and are the perfect alternative for those interested in something other than curtains. Blinds are designed with fabric tape ladders available in a wide selection of colors that can be used to match your color scheme.

Decorative accessories in the living room might include wooden or pewter candlesticks, baskets filled with flowers, family photos in polished wood frames, quilts, and quilted toss pillows. A Shaker framed print of the tree of life might be the perfect addition above the mantel. A painted cupboard can serve as an ideal display case for a collection of stoneware, pewter dishware, or wooden objects. And a Shaker-style painted step stool might come in handy for showcasing flowers and plants. In the living room, the Shaker pegboard can be used for hanging favorite objects.

Dining room furniture with a Shaker country air includes beautiful wood pedestal tables with arched legs forming a tripod base, drop-leaf tables with tapered legs, or long trestle tables with bead-board ends, which were often

Opposite: Just as the Shakers often designed furnishings and spaces to serve more than one purpose, this dining room functions as a place for meals and as a sitting room when the drop-leaf table is placed against the wall. A neutral backdrop shows select furnishings and accessories to their best advantage, such as the hooked rug that becomes wall art. Note, too, how a simple curtain at the window and an old-fashioned braided rug add strong country appeal. A one-of-a-kind coffee table (perhaps used long ago by a tradesman of some sort) puts a personal stamp on this handsome room.
Above: Austere beauty is the end result in this dining room. The wall treatment is reminiscent of a typical Shaker room and sets off the rustic cross-buck table and ladder-back chairs. A metal chandelier is situated above the table for ambiance when dining, and a collection of stoneware is housed in an antique bucket bench that becomes a pleasing focal point.

made with wooden wheels so that they could easily be moved about the room. Shaker slat-back armchairs and side chairs are good additions to a handsome cherry, maple, or other hardwood table. Additional furnishings that might be used in the dining room include a Shaker-style serving table, painted country cupboards, a lovely built-in storage or china cupboard, or perhaps painted benches instead of chairs.

For decorative accessories in the dining room consider a colorful braided rug situated just underneath the table, a metal chandelier (or perhaps a simple but lovely wooden chandelier) above the table for lighting, and pewter-finished wall sconces for ambiance as well as style. A pegboard can also be used to hang candles, baskets, and dried flowers. Create a table setting using woven place mats and simple white pottery or pewter dishware. Woodenware and stoneware will also contribute Shaker country style.

The Shaker Bedroom

The Shaker bedroom was minimally furnished with a bed, a built-in storage cupboard, a washstand, and perhaps a chair or two. A pegboard on the wall was used to hang a small wood-framed mirror and perhaps caps and other articles of clothing. The Shaker bedroom was austere, yes, but it was serene in its simplicity. To create the same sense of style in today's country bedroom, consider painting walls a cream color and using bayberry, teal, blue, or perhaps maroon for door and window trim. Paint a pegboard to match for a unified look. And remember that a wood floor can be accessorized with a braided, rag, or needlepoint rug for added comfort underfoot. The modern look of wall-to-wall carpeting can always be softened by layering rugs atop

Above: Inspired by the fine craftsmanship and simple design of Shaker furnishings, a clean-lined four-poster bed is the center of attention in this private sanctuary. A colorful quilt is all that's needed as a bed dressing, and decorative touches, such as white homespun curtains, an oval braided rug, and even a spinning wheel, contribute a personal country feel.

the carpet. Once your background has been designed to your taste you can turn

your attention to bedroom furnishings.

Shaker-style beds were crafted with a simple headboard (and head posts)

and low foot posts. Reproductions of this style are being made today in sizes

ranging from twin to queen. Other beds would be suitable in a Shaker-inspired

Above: Shaker design can be introduced into any room through small but significant details. The formality of an elaborate Victorian bed is tempered by country accents
such as a Shaker pegboard for articles of clothing, a metal chandelier, and a casual
ladder-back chair. The checkered pattern of the blanket at the foot of the bed is repeated in the lampshade on the bedside table for an added dash of country.

Shaker Oval Pantry Boxes

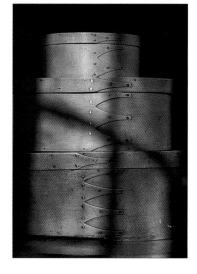

* Shaker boxes are handcrafted of wood and constructed with overlapping "fingers."

* Boxes can be completed with a wood finish or painted in various shades of red, yellow, blue, and green.

* Boxes made in graduated sizes (at least twelve different sizes) can be used in the kitchen and for storing sewing supplies.

* These boxes are designed to nest one inside the other, thus proving to be functional and simple. They are ideal for use throughout the Shaker country home.

* Antique examples can be quite costly depending upon size, color, and condition, but reproductions are far less expensive.

rocker will not only provide a spot to relax but give the bedroom a real touch of Shaker style.

Since window dressings in the bedroom are often necessary to control natural light, a simple curtain might be joined by a shade that can be pulled down as needed. Neutral-colored tab or tailored curtains can also be lined for practicality or can be purchased in a deep shade that will match the room's decor. Wood blinds or even shutters can also be used in the bedroom, where their texture and crisp lines enhance a simple decorating scheme.

The bedroom is actually a refuge of sorts and not just a place to rest your head, so by all means personalize this private space. Family photos, books, flowers, and cherished treasures are all at home in today's Shaker-inspired bedroom. And don't forget to dress your bed for comfort. A warm quilt or coverlet will recall nineteenth-century spirit while a colored comforter will convey a cozy, easy style. Add a wool throw to the foot of the bed for afternoon naps and keep a toss pillow or two close by.

bedroom provided that they meet the requirements: they must be plain and simple. For example, a four-poster bed with tapered posts or even a metal bed that's been painted are just a couple of possibilities. Even an antique or contemporary brass bed can be juxtaposed with Shaker furnishings and still convey a strong sense of country style.

Plain furnishings (without decorative moldings, hardware, or embellishment) such as maple or cherry dressers and chests of drawers are in keeping with the spirit of Shaker style; simple, painted case pieces can also be used. Add a Shaker tape-seat bench or a blanket box at the foot of the bed. Round or rectangular-top candle stands can be used as bedside tables. And a Shaker chair or

The Shaker Kitchen

The kitchen and the bathroom can be very pleasing environments when decorated in a Shaker country style. In the kitchen, where cabinetry becomes a focal point, choose cupboards with plain lines and no noticeable architectural trim. Wood-tone cabinets in cherry, maple, birch, or pine with plain wood pulls are perfect. Cabinetry can be custom-made in the Shaker style, or you can check home building centers and specialty showrooms for a good idea of what's available in stock cabinetry.

And while a wood finish can add natural beauty to the kitchen, painted cabinets are also a popular choice in the Shaker country home. After planning a

color scheme you may decide your kitchen cabinets should be painted mustard, deep green, dark red, bayberry, gray, or brown. Once again, it's a matter of personal taste and how you wish to express Shaker country style.

A gleaming wood countertop continues the simplicity theme. A white laminate counter blends beautifully with wood or painted wood cabinetry. Hardwood or vinyl flooring with a traditional checkered pattern are ideal for this interpretation of a country kitchen.

Furnishings in the Shaker country kitchen can include a trestle table and tape-seat chairs for casual family meals or perhaps reproduction weaver's chairs pulled up to a kitchen counter for snacks and light meals. The weaver's chair, a classic marriage of design and utility, was used by Shaker sisters working at their hand looms, and combines the height of a stool and the grace of a chair with a low slat-back for support. Other furnishings might include a storage cupboard—freestanding or built into a wall, either of which could be cus-

Above left: This small kitchen pantry is big on Shaker style, courtesy of the bayberry-colored dry sink and choice examples of redware pottery on display. For good measure, country accents such as carved ducks, a lovely basket, and a needlepoint rug have been added.

Above right: A late 1800s kitchen boasts simple Shaker influence in its plank flooring, plain painted walls, and basic window treatment. An oval braided rug defines space for a handsome drop-leaf table and chairs while an antique dry sink sits before the window. A beautiful desk keeps family paperwork close at hand and an iron cookstove with an innovative hot-water tank stands in front of a brick hearth.

tom-crafted—an antique or reproduction step-back cupboard, or a Shaker dry sink.

For lighting, think wood or metal. A chandelier above the kitchen table and sufficient lighting for work areas are a must. Recessed lighting can be both practical and unobtrusive for the countertop area where cooking and baking are prepared, while a beautiful chandelier that imparts simple country style can take center stage in the open areas.

As in the other rooms of the Shaker country home, simple curtains will work best to flavor the kitchen's style. Depending on your color scheme you may want something other than natural muslin curtains—maybe a soft plaid, a gingham, or an old-fashioned calico print. Any of these speak of country spirit, but keep in mind that ruffles may be a bit too much for this style. Opt instead for tailored, tab, or pinch-pleat curtains, or a simple valance.

Practical and decorative accessories in the kitchen include everything from wooden bowls, which can be used for holding fruit or serving tossed salad; wood-

Above: Simplicity is paramount as natural elements and a low-key color scheme infuse this modern kitchen with Shaker country style. White walls and cabinets blend beautifully with a wood floor and countertop. A glass-front pantry cupboard shows off a collection of white ironstone pottery, baskets, and dishware. Even the counter pays tribute to country style by gathering utensils together in a crock and displaying fruit in baskets. Against the wall, a child's high chair sports the clean lines of Shaker design.

enware utensils; stoneware jugs, pitchers, crocks, and tableware; and Shaker oval pantry boxes. Other ideas for decorative touches in the kitchen include hanging a pegboard and using it to hang pots and pans or to display an assortment of Shaker brooms, dried herbs and flowers, and baskets. On walls you may want to consider hanging a collection of cheese baskets with a hexagon-shaped

The Shaker Bathroom

You can give the bathroom a pleasing dose of Shaker style by drawing from the appropriate color palette in designing the room's backdrop. Cream walls can be accented with a trim color; window and door frames can be stained with a wood finish. A wood, tile, or vinyl floor can be accessorized with a scatter rug for clear-cut country style.

Regardless of how modern the bath appears, you can still create a sense of the style by introducing furnishings and accessories that make a strong statement. For example, a Shaker chair or bench—whether for seating or stacking towels—will set the tone for your country decor. Consider, too, a freestanding Shaker towel rack for bathroom linens. A plain wood-framed mirror above the sink or vanity will continue the theme of simplicity. For extra storage space a pegboard can be hung on a bathroom wall for robes or towels, and you can make use of oval Shaker boxes for soaps and toiletries.

Lighting in the bath can take the form of a plain ceiling fixture sporting an unadorned glass globe (white or clear) and clean-lined matching wall sconces on either side of the mirror. Wood or metal-trimmed lighting fixtures are also available, so select those fixtures that appeal to your sense of country style.

For curtains in the bath, a simple tailored look is fine. Fabrics should be selected with easy care in mind and perhaps coordinated with the shower curtain. Striped ticking or a neutral shade such as cream or beige will complement a Shaker country theme.

As with any interpretation of country style, you want to make each room inviting and comfortable as well as practical. In true Shaker spirit the country home's function is surpassed only by its beauty.

weave or a reproduction Shaker Seed Company poster. The key is to limit decorative accessories to those select few you feel most strongly convey your sense of Shaker country style. If there are too many collections or items on display, the inherent simplicity of Shaker style will get lost in the mix.

Above: Collections on display are the very heart and soul of country style. Nineteenth-century tinware is showcased on unadorned shelves. The timbered ceiling and bayberry-colored plank wall make the perfect setting for this vintage kitchenware collection. Something as inspired as a mason jar filled with flowers makes the decor spring to life.

Chapter Five

Country Victorian

Country as a state of mind was a concept the Victorians took to heart—and then took one step further with summer retreats to seaside cottages, country homes, and vacation lodges. For the nineteenth-century Victorians, harmony with nature took on new meaning and importance as they strove to escape—if just for a short while—growing cities, rapid industrialization, and the strict formality of everyday life. Harmony with nature, in fact, became a key consideration in home building during the mid-1800s, which noted horticulturist and architect Andrew Jack-

son Downing conveyed in his 1850 plan book, *The Architecture of Country Houses*. Downing was of the opinion, and many Victorians concurred, that the home should be "enriched without and within by objects of universal interest." And what could provide more universal interest than Mother Nature herself?

Whether located in the city or rural areas, the Victorian home was genteel and refined. Ah, but the vacation homes and small cottages of the middle class—these were often decorated in a style far less formal than the city house and in such a way that a carefree spirit and love of nature

Above: *The tabletop array is a hallmark of Victorian style and happily the credo seems to be "the more the merrier." The fringe-bedecked round table makes a fitting display surface for a collection of antique magnifying glasses and framed photos. A lovely decanter and stemware await visitors. An informal arrangement of dried flowers adds a light, country touch in this Victorian display.* *Opposite:* *A country Victorian setting can be every bit as elegant as a more formal, uptown Victorian Revival style. Lighter wood tones and pale rather than dark hues create a fresh new color scheme that is casual, yet refined. A handsome four-poster bed incorporates an eye-catching use of fabric designed as a canopy and the bed is most definitely dressed for opulent comfort. A striking table used as a bedside stand allows room for the perfect finishing touch—a white pitcher filled with tulips.*

were apparent everywhere. This is the style we've come to know as country Victorian—a decorating scheme that combines a tempered measure of Victoriana and a good dose of country comfort and spirit with a touch of romance. Romance? Without a doubt, country Victorian does indeed have a subtle, romantic air—how could it not, with lace, chintz, and treasured collectibles as hallmarks of this appealing style?

The country Victorian home of long ago brought the outdoors inside—nature in all her glory was celebrated on everything from wallpapers and rugs to dishware and decorative bric-a-brac. Architectural embellishment was sometimes—but not always—scaled back or less massive than in the formal city home. For example, resort and oceanside cottages displayed pastel colors, a profusion of gingerbread trim, and fanciful, even whimsical historical references, such as turrets. Furniture, too, tended to be lighter in color and materials, suitable to warmer weather and smaller household staffs.

Country Victorian Colors at a Glance

pink	pastel blue	pastel green	lavender	beige
light gray	buff	cream	rose	pastel yellow

Country Victorian Colors and Patterns

Colors in the country Victorian home tended to be lighter and brighter than the muted shades in vogue during the late 1800s. Pastels and even neutral shades made rooms airy and inviting. Furnishings displayed texture, as with wicker, or homey comfort and appeal, found in the upholstered pieces given new life in a second home or simply handed down from one family member to the next. To complete the decorative scheme, accessories were practical as well as attractive but certainly not highbrow. Pottery was preferred over china, as chintz was over damask, and seashells and driftwood often replaced the silver candlesticks on the mantelpiece.

Just as vibrant colors and French Provençal fabrics are hallmarks of the French country style, and twig furnishings are synonymous with rustic adaptations, rich patterns and wicker furnishings are most certainly trademarks of country Victorian style. For example, the more casual Victorian home often made use of wallpapers bedecked with floral motifs, especially the rose. A cabbage rose pattern was a favorite during the Victorian age, but so, too, were smaller prints (mini prints) and petite florals combined with geometric patterns. Other flowers and leaves also found their way onto charming wallpapers, just as birds and animals did. In the rural country home, middle-class cottage, or vacation retreat, wallpapers generally featured lighter colors and delicate patterns that enhanced but did not dominate any given room.

Wallpaper really came into its own as a decorating tool during the nineteenth century, and even the most humble household or informal retreat was not immune to its charms. During the early 1800s wallpaper was produced using carved pearwood blocks to create patterns in a process known as block printing, and the majority of wallpapers put to use in the United States were

imported from England and France. Although a wallpaper factory was established in New York City as early as 1765, many years elapsed before the industry grew large enough in the States to meet the demand. With the invention of a wallpaper-printing machine in the early 1800s the industry finally flourished,

and by the 1860s several dozen firms located in America's large cities were turning out wallpapers in assorted colors and styles. While there were stylized floral motifs associated with the Art Nouveau movement of the late nineteenth century and certainly the nature-inspired patterns of the Arts and Crafts

Above left: Country Victorian style pays tribute to nature by bringing souvenirs of the great outdoors inside. This mantel is a study in simplicity and beauty thanks to a collection of starfish and seashells. The framed seascape on the wall reinforces the open-air theme and becomes a fitting focal point.

Above right: A delicate toile de Jouy wallpaper provides the perfect backdrop for this garden-inspired bedroom. The same flowered fabric is used for the curtains and comforter cover, bouquets of real blooms continue the floral theme, and a buttery yellow color scheme blends harmoniously with the warm wood tones of the furnishings and picture frames.

Above: *A lovely painted bed featuring a headboard embellished with a pastel floral motif and festoons becomes the focus of this country Victorian bedroom. Wicker furnishings—in this case a cushioned chaise lounge and a comfy settee—are ideal in a relaxed setting. The timbered ceiling adds a provincial country touch while art-glass window inserts pay homage to Victorian design. The end result? The best of both decorative worlds blended beautifully into one.*

period, there were also myriad other designs that appealed to the country folk and were appropriate for simpler decorating schemes.

Country Victorian Furniture

Along with nature-inspired patterns, country Victorian decorating calls to mind airy wicker furnishings—perhaps updated with a coat of crisp, white paint and comfy cushions. Wicker, in fact, has been used in the home since before the mid-1800s but didn't reach a high point in popularity until the 1880s. Prior to 1860, wicker pieces were being imported from the Far East and England but by 1855 Cyrus Wakefield had founded the Wakefield Rattan Company in South Reading, Massachusetts, and before long others in the United States followed suit. This early wicker furniture was made from cane fashioned around hardwood frames and was either varnished or painted in then-popular colors such as green, white, or black.

Wicker has actually been a generic term used for years to describe furniture made of cane, reed, rattan, willow, and paper fiber. This last category was made possible during the early 1900s with the invention of a machine called the Lloyd loom, which could produce sheets of woven paper fiber that were then wrapped around a furniture frame. The

wicker furnishings produced by the Lloyd Manufacturing Company were mostly used indoors, since they weren't as weather-resistant as their "natural" counterparts made of reed, cane, and rattan.

Styles of wicker furniture kept pace with the times. During the late 1800s fashionable pieces, used on the front porch as well as indoors, were decorative and ornate, with curlicues, elaborate designs, and all manner of trimwork. By the turn of the century the trend toward streamlining interiors saw wicker furniture being manufactured with a toned-down open latticework design that was especially popular at resort hotels and vacation lodges as well as in

middle-class homes. Collectors today will often refer to this particular style as Bar Harbor wicker furniture. The Arts and Crafts movement also exercised a stylistic influence on wicker furnishings. Simplicity reigned supreme in the closed-weave, rectangular wicker furniture produced from the early 1900s to the 1920s. Outfitted with comfortable cushions, these wicker pieces blended beautifully with the handsome Mission oak furnishings that became a mainstay of the bungalow architectural style.

A wide variety of wicker furniture was produced from the late 1800s to about 1930, including several kinds of chairs, rockers, settees, sofas, tables,

Above left: The rugged, outdoorsy texture of a wicker tabletop is beautiful left just as is. Cherished treasures are given a choice spot and arranged in a pleasing medley. Casual country Victorian spirit reigns supreme.

Above right: An exuberant bouquet atop a white wicker table speaks of simple elegance. A collection of blue and white dishware, a universal favorite during the nineteenth century, makes an eye-catching wall display. A neutral background allows the hues of these decorative touches to take center stage.

dining room furniture, lamps, desks, whatnot stands, music stands, tea carts, children's furniture, sewing baskets, plant stands, bedroom dressers, and even Victrolas. These and other wicker items for the home were manufactured during the late nineteenth century not only by the Wakefield Rattan Company but also by Heywood Brothers and Company. These two giants of the industry merged in 1897 to form the Heywood Brothers and Wakefield Rattan Compa-

ny, and by 1921 the Lloyd Manufacturing Company also became a part of this firm. Many other, smaller companies also turned out wicker furniture in the United States, including Joseph P. McHugh and Company of New York City, the Prairie Grass Furniture Company of Glendale, New York, the Charles Schober Company of Philadelphia, and the Boston Willow Furniture Company of Boston, Massuchusetts.

Above left: Look beyond the tabletop display composed of flower arrangements and decorative floral china to the lovely blue walls, which have been accented with white trim. The private expanse of the secluded back yard makes no window dressing the best possible dressing of all.

Above right: A blooming delight, this stunning living room features a pastel color scheme and floral chintz upholstery on the plump sofa and overstuffed easy chairs. An Oriental rug defines space and showcases a one-of-a-kind coffee table composed of architectural salvage and a simple glass top. A Victorian screen acts as artwork and a generous supply of bric-a-brac, books, pillows, and flowers creates a quintessential country Victorian setting. Note, too, the architecture of the recessed shelves filled with the owner's collection of majolica pottery pieces.

By the early 1930s the modern style displaced wicker, and many companies closed or turned their attention elsewhere. Fortunately much antique wicker is still available, as are quality reproductions that are perfect for outfitting or accessorizing the country Victorian home. When hunting for antique wicker, check antiques shops, shows, and auctions. Inspect pieces carefully to determine condition and sound construction. Purchase rare or costly pieces from a dealer specializing in vintage furniture and be aware that repairs can be quite expensive.

The essence of country Victorian style also was, and still is, conveyed with bamboo furnishings, cast-iron pieces painted white, chintz-upholstered furniture, and collections or single pieces of bric-a-brac such as majolica pottery, floral prints, shell-covered boxes and picture frames, and of course fresh flowers, plants, warm throws, and comfy toss pillows.

The Country Victorian Entryway

Today's country Victorian style appeals to many because it can be dressed up or down to achieve a casual or even a semiformal air while still conveying comfort, warmth, and old-fashioned charm. For example, the front hall or entryway can be made inviting with a soft pastel color accented with white trim. For a somewhat dressy look add a floral wallpaper border or stencil design near the ceiling, or create a dado/field effect by combining a bead-board wainscot with a painted or paper top-half of entryway walls. Small floral patterns or mini prints delightfully express country Victorian charm.

A tile or wood floor in the casual entry can be accessorized with a colorful rag rug or a floral needlepoint rug. For bold country spirit, try mixing a traditional checkered tile floor (white and black, white and blue, or white and

green) with a subtle floral wallpaper that hints at Victoriana. Don't despair if your home is decked out with wall-to-wall carpeting—simply place a decorative area rug atop the carpet for stylish impact as well as practical purposes (it preserves the carpet).

Furnishings and decorative accessories in the front hall can include an antique or reproduction hall tree, which is ideal for providing space to hang coats, hats, and purses. There are vintage golden oak examples as well as cast-iron models that are striking when given a coat of white paint. Decorative hooks can also suffice for hanging outdoor gear, or a brass coat rack will do

Above: Color, pattern, and texture reminiscent of a lush flower garden have been drawn together to design a cozy, country Victorian living room corner. A floral print sofa with an abundance of pillows is accompanied by a natural-finish wicker chair. A rustic bench finds new life as a coffee table and sports a hooked-rug throw. Beside the sofa an ornate whatnot shelf provides space for family photos and a colorful lamp. Even a vintage suitcase becomes a furnishing of sorts beside the family's collection of compact discs.

quite nicely. Add a small table if room allows—wicker, bamboo, or an odd table that's been rescued and restored with decorative paint. Add a painted bench, a wicker chair, or an old-fashioned trunk and accessorize with a beautiful hanging light fixture sporting a colored glass, art glass, or frosted glass shade. A pottery umbrella holder, a basket or jardinière full of flowers, and lace panels at a window or sidelights are perfect finishing touches. Your entry will most definitely say, "Welcome to my country Victorian home."

The Country Victorian Living Room

The living room and dining room, by virtue of their nature as the public rooms in the house, have long been the focus of decorative details. The country Victorian parlor of a century ago was a careful blend of upholstered furnishings and outdoor textures such as wicker, which contributed a casual mood and subtle informality to a room created for family and friends. The same still holds true today. For the perfect backdrop select your favorite pastels or soft shades of color for paint or paper to create ambiance. And don't overlook white or neutral shades: they can be the perfect way to let furnishings take center stage. You can also use ragging or sponging techniques for a more spirited painted wall. For devoted fans of wallpaper, small floral designs, mini prints, stripes, or a geometric diamond motif are all in keeping with a country Victorian setting. Keep in mind that a pastel or neutral color scheme will add light to a room but a large space may call for deeper shades to make it cozy and inviting.

Many country homeowners enjoy the comfort and ease of wall-to-wall carpeting, and in the country Victorian parlor or living room this can be an especially nice touch. You can select a rugged, textured carpet to contribute country flair or a softly patterned carpet for more romantic appeal. A large

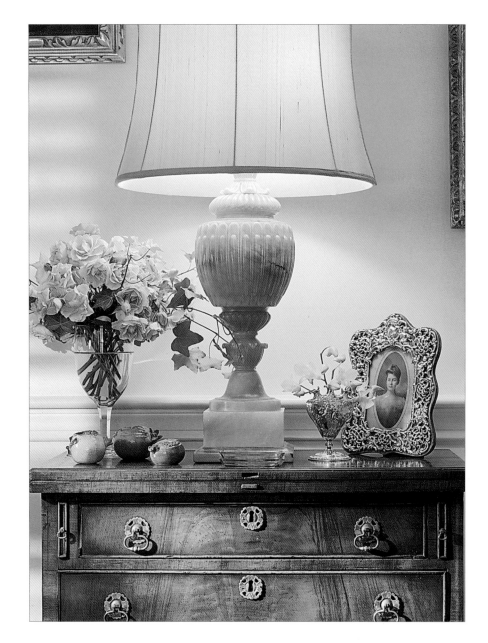

Above: A romantic, semiformal air is achieved in this picture-perfect country Victorian setting. A period dresser supports a simple yet elegant marble lamp, a silver-framed picture, and a beautiful bouquet of fresh roses. Opposite: A blue and white chintz-covered easy chair and matching ottoman create an inviting place to relax. Potted tulips, candlelight, and a good book leave just one option—curling up for a lazy afternoon. Country Victorian spirit is apparent not only in the furnishings and pleasing color scheme, but in the careful attention to small, decorative details.

Wall and flooring treatments will help set the tone for this interpretation of country style, but when it comes to designing the background, architectural embellishment cannot be overlooked. A fireplace—the quintessential symbol of a warm and inviting home—can become a focal point in the country Victorian living room whether it wears a mantel of gleaming golden oak or has been updated with a fresh coat of paint. Decorative touches such as an eye-catching tile border, a vintage fire screen, and even treasured collectibles on the mantelshelf make it that much more appealing. Consider, too, the use of other architectural features such as a simple but lovely cornice; door and window moldings; brass, glass, or porcelain doorknobs; and even an art glass window or two.

Furniture and decorative accessories at home in the living room that are an effective blend of Victoriana and good old-fashioned country style include upholstered pieces (sofas and easy chairs) with sink-down comfort and an ottoman that can serve as a footrest, as extra seating, or even as a coffee table. Select fabrics that convey a free and easy spirit, such as floral chintz, striped ticking, or perhaps a cheerful checkered design. Just imagine how lovely a Victorian wood-trimmed settee or sofa can be when juxtaposed with a bright checkered pattern. And don't forget lots of throw pillows—the plumper the better, with braided trim rather than the more formal fringe and tassels.

expanse of solid-colored carpet can naturally be accessorized with area rugs to define furniture groupings or focal points. Area rugs are also a good way to protect and decorate a hardwood or plank wood floor. Floral or geometric needlepoints, colorful rag rugs, and even a wonderful Oriental rug are all suitable choices for a country Victorian theme.

To complete the living room, add a wicker rocker or chairs with comfortable cushions, use an old steamer trunk as a coffee table, and put that bamboo whatnot shelf to use as a mini bookcase or display case for favorite collectibles. Painted pieces such as a step-back cupboard, a blanket chest, or even a vintage bench can serve a multitude of purposes.

Above: Any living room fireplace commands attention but this example is especially striking. A fresh coat of white paint enhances the architectural design and allows the fireplace to blend with white walls sporting decorative moldings. The manteltop becomes a display shelf for select pottery while a framed botanical print draws the eye upward. Lovely upholstered furnishings, an attractive area rug, and a fabric window shade complete this country Victorian–inspired setting.

To complement your country Victorian decor, windows should be dressed with light draperies, shutters, or airy lace panels. A beautiful swag or valance can also impart casual, romantic style. The secret is to create an attractive yet informal treatment that will make windows appear decorative, not heavy-handed. In a sense the same can also be said of lighting. While a crystal chandelier is definitely too highbrow for a casual country Victorian theme, a

Above: Clustering appealing pieces or collections is a hallmark of country Victorian style. An ivy topiary in a natural clay pot mingles quite nicely with favorite objects, framed photos, an architectural fragment, and an heirloom candlestick.

The Elements of Country Victorian Style

❋ Comfortable upholstered furnishings, wicker furniture, painted cupboards, benches, and chairs

❋ Bamboo furnishings

❋ Cast-iron hall trees

❋ Floral patterns, floral chintz fabrics, and lace

❋ Nature-inspired accessories made with shells and flowers

❋ Antiques and collectibles such as majolica pottery, white ironstone, floral painted china, decorative tins, and kitchenware items such as yellowware bowls

Above: Country Victorian ambiance awaits dinner guests. A painted timbered ceiling and geometric floral wallpaper create a pleasing, romantic backdrop. An Oriental rug plays host to a handsome round table and assorted wicker chairs. A large, glass-front armoire makes a beautiful china cupboard with lace-edged shelves. Note, too, how this inviting setting is imbued with romance by the simple addition of a lace-edged chandelier.

hanging fixture with a hand-painted globe and delicate glass prisms might be just right. Also consider antique or reproduction lamps with art glass shades, wicker lamps, student lamps, or lovely pottery-based lamps. When a fabric shade is called for, a floral or striped print can add pattern while a solid color may be preferred to enhance a color scheme. It's purely a matter of choice and personal taste.

It goes without saying that country Victorian style derives a great deal of its charm from antiques, collectibles, and cherished treasures put to their best advantage on display. Whether your passion is old botanical prints, majolica pottery, brass candlesticks, heirloom picture frames, small trinkets, books, hand-painted china, or baskets, you can compose delightful arrangements, attractive wallscapes, or glass-front cupboards artistically cluttered for visual appeal. As always, add fresh flowers and lush green plants to enhance the spirit of nature and the outdoors.

The Country Victorian Dining Room

The country Victorian dining room can be made every bit as warm and welcoming as the living room by creating the ideal frame through the use of paint, wallpaper, restrained architectural embellishment, and decorative rugs or a gleaming hardwood floor. Actually, in many Victorian homes of the past, the colors used in the dining room echoed those in the parlor; they were simply used in reverse. This is a decorative idea that still has merit today, especially in an open floor plan or a home where the dining room can be entered from the living room.

To keep the dining room from becoming too formal or stuffy—to actually create a room you'll use regularly rather than just on special occasions—

furnish it casually and comfortably. You want your dining room to invite people to linger over coffee and relaxed conversation. With this in mind, a wicker table and cushioned chairs might suit you just fine. If, however, you adore the warmth of wood, a gleaming oak, cherry, or pinewood table will be ideal. A gate-leg, drop-leaf, round, or rectangular table—or even a long harvest table—can be outfitted with Windsor chairs, ladder-back chairs, pressed-back chairs, or casual but elegant upholstered chairs.

If the size of your dining space allows it, add a china cabinet where dishware can be displayed or perhaps a vintage sideboard for storage space. Hang pottery plates in a decorative arrangement on the wall or showcase your favorite artwork using handsome frames. A gilt mirror above the mantel (if you're fortunate enough to have a fireplace in the dining room) is an excellent way to reflect light back across the room, and candlelight is always a favorite for evoking the spirit of days gone by. It's the little things that can have big impact: the table set with crisp, white linens and pottery plates, fresh flowers casually arranged in an ironstone jug, a beautiful fern poised by the window in a wicker planter, or a window swag that just happens to match the fabric used on the chair cushions.

The Country Victorian Bedroom

The romantic appeal of country Victorian style is perhaps at its best in the bedroom. Truly a personal sanctuary, the bedroom can be dressed up or down as you see fit. The country Victorian bedroom can be in full bloom with a lovely floral wallpaper, or a more subdued approach can be taken with walls painted in soothing pastel colors. By adding a wallpaper border or a stencil design you can enjoy a combination of decorative effects.

The floor in this private retreat can be rather spartan, such as a simple wood floor with a scatter rug or two, or plush underfoot with thick wall-to-wall carpet. Either is fine, although carpet has the definite advantage of reducing sound. Carpeting, in fact, can add dramatic flair if a deep shade is chosen to complement pastel walls and soft trim. Remember that casual comfort is the key.

For furnishing the country Victorian bedroom there are actually several old-fashioned designs that will impart the desired informal style. Wicker is a natural, and a lovely bed as well as a dresser or chest of drawers will immediately convey casual Victorian ease. Cottage furniture—those appealing painted

Above: Sun filtering through the bedroom window captures the dreamy appeal of this country Victorian bedroom. An opulent brass bed is layered with lacy linens and a patterned spread while antique lace has been fashioned into an overhead canopy. The neutral color scheme combines a floral wallpaper with a simple yet elegant window treatment. For decorative appeal an ornate iron planter has been filled with white blooms.

style enthusiasts. Other possibilities include a white iron bed, a brass bed, a handsome four-poster bed, or even a beautiful canopy bed complete with lace or soft, billowing fabric.

Storage pieces for the bedroom can be a "suite" of matching pieces or a medley of chests that have found new life together, such as a pine chest of drawers or a vintage cherry dresser. Castoffs from an earlier time can even be painted for a unified look and then used in tandem with a painted blanket box or a provincial-style armoire. Add a bedside table and a comfortable chair or two—whatever makes you feel most at home.

Decorative accessories can be practical or pure whimsy. Lighting needs must be met, whether you use antique fixtures with exquisite art glass shades or modern reproductions with the look of days gone by. A ceiling fixture with a frosted or etched glass shade as well as a bedside lamp or two—perhaps with a crafted pottery base and cabbage-rose fabric shade—can add a decorative touch. Bedroom windows, too, can be dressed with myriad treatments that are both functional and offer a measure of country Victorian style. Lace panels, chintz curtains, Priscilla curtains (with delicate ruffles), painted shutters, or even a beautiful valance or swag (with a shade to be used as needed) will com-

pieces turned out during the late nineteenth century—are also well suited to a romantic bedroom. Bedecked with delicate floral sprays, spool turnings, and soft pastel colors, these vintage furnishings are increasingly sought by country

Above: This beautiful bedroom has it all—a white iron bed with brass trim and a generous amount of bedding, subtle, striped walls with a matching window dressing, and a floral wallpaper border used as a Victorian accent. The window treatment incorporates both shutters and a shade to control natural lighting and allow privacy. A desk does double duty as a bedside stand, and a low dresser allows for a large, ornate mirror. A framed botanical print, fresh flowers, and masses of inviting pillows on the bed enhance the country Victorian decorating scheme.

plement the decor. Also consider bamboo or matchstick shades, which add a relaxed, rustic texture and subtle hints of the great outdoors.

Surround yourself with those objects that bring you pleasure such as warm quilts or comforters, framed prints, family photos, fresh flowers, books, throw

pillows, and favorite keepsakes. Your dresser top might be home to a collection of antique toiletry bottles and jars, or perhaps you've assembled a collection of shell-studded boxes. With the best of both styles at hand—simple country and romantic Victorian—your bedroom can be beautiful.

Above left: An antique cottage-style dresser is the perfect addition to this country Victorian bedroom. Crafted of pine or poplar, this piece exhibits stenciled detailing and painted floral motifs. Sitting atop it are matching lamps with ribboned shades. Nature-inspired framed prints, a handsome, country-style mirror, a brass bed, and floral wallpaper—everything comes together effortlessly in this cozy sanctuary.

Above right: Simple beauty is created by dressing this bed with a delicately arced white canopy, a lace-edged dust ruffle, and a colorful quilt. Wallpaper and wide plank floors outfitted with needlepoint rugs convey the casual spirit of a country Victorian decor while a more formally classical chest of drawers and mirror imbue the room with a dash of traditional style.

The Country Victorian Kitchen and Bathroom

Function and modern-day convenience are uppermost when it comes to the kitchen and bath. Fortunately the Victorian interpretation of country style allows ample opportunity to combine no-nonsense practicality with casual, attractive style in either room. Take, for example, the kitchen, where contemporary, state-of-the-art appliances reside alongside cabinets and counters that serve up the quintessential expression of the style. The secret is to call upon the materials of the past—materials that have proven themselves decorative as well as durable for years. Tile is the perfect example. It's a wonderful choice for flooring, countertops, and even walls. After your color scheme for the kitchen has been decided, look to colorful or artistic tiles to infuse the room with your own personal rendition of country Victorian style. You may decide on a floor done in traditional checks or opt for something with a simple floral design. With tile your choices are limitless.

The countertop can be composed of tiles of a single color, such as emerald green, white, or deep blue, or a pattern can be designed. Tile can also serve as a backsplash in the countertop area or behind the stove. Savvy collectors and creative homeowners often seek out antique tiles with patterns and create one-of-a-kind arrangements on a kitchen wall behind the stove. And while tile certainly is not the only option when it comes to kitchen counters (there are also woods and laminates to be considered), it does afford the most leeway in terms of creative design for the country Victorian kitchen.

Tile is very well suited for flooring in that it's durable, easy to maintain, and comes in a wide variety of colors, sizes, and patterns. It can, however, be costly if your kitchen is large. An alternative possibility that will evoke a country Victorian spirit is a wood or vinyl floor that offers the look of tile, and also

Opposite: Reminiscent of a cozy Victorian cottage, this kitchen charmingly illustrates how collectibles can contribute decorative effects. Pale blue walls provide a background for windows trimmed in white and treated to simple lace valances. A skirted sink becomes a focal point courtesy of a deep-shaded floral fabric. Glass bottles on a display shelf near the ceiling, a whimsical birdcage hung in the corner, fresh flowers, framed prints, tea towels, and assorted china create artistic and appealing clutter.

Above: Older kitchen cabinetry is updated with cream-colored paint and then embellished with brass pulls and floral stenciled designs to evoke country Victorian spirit. A warm, wood floor, wearing the lovely patina acquired over time, is a favorite option for flooring. Small but significant accents, such as the glass jars atop the counter, add casual country appeal.

Majolica Pottery

* Majolica is earthenware with molded decorations that are slip-coated and then painted with a colored lead glaze.

* Majolica was made in England, the United States, and throughout Europe from the mid-1800s to the early 1900s.

* Majolica features whimsical floral, foliage, fruit, vegetable, and animal motifs.

* Common items include platters, plates, cups and saucers, oyster plates, bowls, pitchers, teapots, planters, jardinières, candlesticks, vases, and novelty items.

* A sampling of well-known manufacturers includes Griffen, Smith & Company in America, Minton Porcelain Manufacturing Company in England, and Sarreguemines in France.

* Marked pieces fetch more in the antiques market than unmarked pieces, but many wonderful items produced without markings can still be had for a modest investment. Some marked items can cost several hundred dollars depending upon the particular piece, its rarity, the manufacturer, and the quality of the hand-painted decoration (which was often done by women).

* Several pieces of majolica displayed together can make a striking focal point in a country Victorian setting.

comes in other patterns and designs. Regardless of what you select to meet your needs, a decorative scatter rug or two can be used in the kitchen (especially in work areas) to provide added comfort underfoot.

Kitchen cabinets with lighter wood tones such as a honey pine, warm cherry, or golden oak set a more casual tone than do dark woods, which are

Above: Tile can be ideal on countertops and walls in a country Victorian kitchen or bath. This sink area is not only embellished with a practical and pristine white tile, but a trompe l'oeil painting above the backsplash adds a one-of-a-kind decorative effect that becomes a charming focal point. Art imitates life, thanks to the arrangement of items on the countertop. Last but not least, in keeping with the casual decorating spirit, lace panels have been used at the window.

associated with a more formal decor. A restrained use of moldings, white porcelain knobs, and even glass-front doors are all in keeping with the nature of country Victorian style. Painted cabinetry can also be quite charming, whether it's white or a shade especially developed to blend with your color scheme. Add an old Hoosier cabinet, a step-back cupboard, or a hutch for an authentic touch and the perfect place to display kitchen collectibles.

Recessed lighting can be used for work areas of the country Victorian kitchen, while a more traditonal hanging fixture can draw attention to the kitchen table and spotlight family meals. Select a metal fixture with old-fashioned charm or perhaps a brass light with frosted glass globes. A fixture with a fabric shade can be coordinated with curtain or cushion fabric, or a fabric can be chosen purely for its playful touch. And when it comes to curtains, simple café curtains, tab curtains, or rod-pockets in a striped, floral, or checkered pattern will always do nicely. Lace panels can also be used in the kitchen, as can shutters, decorative fabric, or matchstick shades.

Kitchen collectibles speak volumes when it comes to country Victorian style. Gleaming copper cookware, white ironstone dishware, baskets, antique tins, and kitchenware such as vintage coffee grinders, scales, and ceramic "cereal sets" or canisters (many of which were made in Germany or Czechoslovakia at the turn of the century) are a few suggestions for enhancing your kitchen with simple items of the past.

For the bathroom, country Victorian style can be achieved in a big way by making use of a bead-board wainscot on walls (combined with a wallpaper in your favorite pastel hue), a tile or wood floor, and well-chosen decorative accessories. Add a rag or needlepoint rug to emphasize color, dress the window in an airy lace panel and shade, and select wall sconces and an overhead

fixture that convey your country style. A stunning gilt mirror or perhaps a delicate wicker chair might become a focal point. Floral prints with bamboo frames can be arranged into a pleasing wallscape, while an old-fashioned pedestal sink and claw-foot tub leave no doubt that your bath is rooted in the charm and warmth of this casual nineteenth-century style.

Above: The striking floral striped wallpaper lends this bathroom an unmistakable Victorian flair and a splash of color, which is balanced by the sparkling white sink, walls, and towels. Other country Victorian elements include the collection of bottles and the miniature on a stand, the lush green plants under the sink, and the botanical print on the wall.

Chapter Six

English Charm

Steeped in tradition and firmly rooted in the British countryside, the charms of English country–style decorating have far-reaching appeal. This is a look that has developed over time—a look that resulted not from any deliberate effort to create an interior design style, but rather from the desire to fashion relaxed interiors that complemented the beauty of centuries-old rural settings. Layer upon layer of printed fabrics, soft or slightly elegant window dressings, colorful rugs, comfortable but sturdy furnishings, large honey pine dressers, scrubbed oak tables, hunting and fishing paraphernalia, and decorative accessories and collectibles practically filling a room to overflowing—all are the essence of English country style.

In England during the eighteenth century, country living became increasingly popular among the well-to-do. They devoted time to the manor house and surrounding property through the development of informal gardens and the beauty of natural landscapes. Throughout the 1700s and 1800s the country manor house rivaled the city house in terms of entertaining and socializing.

Above: Part of the appeal of English country style comes from amassing objects with pleasing results. A scenic wallpaper with a mellow, aged look and a gallery-like display of framed family photos make a lovely wallscape. By introducing a small table with matching candlestick lamps and small bouquets of sweet peas, this picture-perfect setting is complete. Opposite: Clearly a look that has developed over time, this warm and inviting living room has the air of a manor house. Upholstered pieces mingle with dark wood tables while Oriental rugs warm the mellow wood floor. Flowers, books, pottery, framed portraits, and even a carved, wooden horse hitched to a small cart are the essence of English country style.

Elegant evening festivities and weekend hunts drew guests and visitors to the lush English countryside in large numbers. Throughout the Victorian age the population in rural areas grew, and while the manor house was indeed the quintessential country home, smaller timber-framed cottages and farmhouses were occupied by the working class and new dwellings were built to satisfy the demands of those seeking a quieter, simpler life that was at one with nature.

While there were indeed vast differences between the manor house and the cozy cottage, they nevertheless shared a common bond when it came to interior design. The rolling green countryside, ancient stone walls, ivy-covered buildings, and flower gardens were the inspiration for the bright or muted shades of color that were popular inside the home. Nature was also the driving

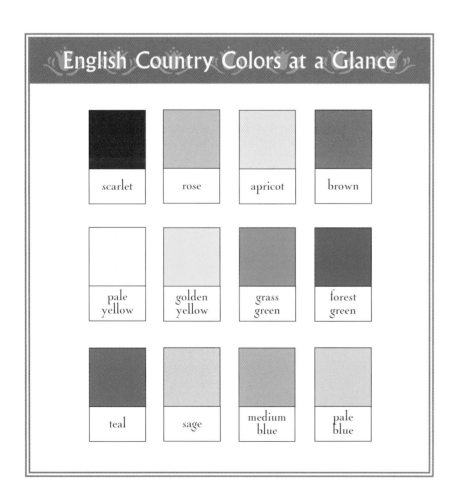

English Country Colors at a Glance

scarlet	rose	apricot	brown
pale yellow	golden yellow	grass green	forest green
teal	sage	medium blue	pale blue

force behind the fine floral fabrics and wallpapers that often teamed up to create an inviting and relaxing atmosphere inside the English country home. Regarding furniture, nothing was tossed out or traded away to be replaced by the latest fashion. Rather, older pieces became family heirlooms that were passed from one generation to the next and never lost their place of honor in the country home. On a more practical note, there were indeed times when

Above: Blending family furniture pieces from different eras is typical of the English country style. Here, a handsome antique table resides alongside a chintz-covered chair with plump toss pillows. A magnificent oil painting and large spray of flowers add aristocratic appeal.

money was tight—even for the wealthy—and families made do with what they had. In the end, this effortless blending of the old, the not so old, and occasionally the new contributed to the essence of English country style.

English Textiles

Creating a country home that conveys a casual English style calls upon some key elements to express this interpretation of country decorating. For example, chintz, especially with small floral designs, is a hallmark of the style. Chintz cotton fabrics originated in India and were exported to England and Europe during the seventeenth century. Colors and patterns were often created with these particular markets in mind, and it wasn't long before chintz became popular for everything from curtains and upholstery to clothing and decorative items.

By the late 1600s textile firms in Great Britain were turning out their own colorful chintz fabrics with floral motifs, and the industry flourished through the nineteenth century. During the early 1900s the glazed cotton fabric often sported designs that featured small-scale floral patterns, ribbons, garlands of roses, and stripes in vibrant colors such as red, yellow, and blue. During the 1930s fashions changed and large floral patterns (roses were quite popular) became the rage. Although fabric and design styles have come and gone throughout the years, chintz never really fell out of fashion, and with today's strong interest in the English country style, chintz has once again taken center

stage. Fabrics and wallpapers with chintz patterns are designed today to create a coordinated look; two or more patterns can be combined for eclectic appeal.

No discussion of chintz fabric would be complete without mentioning the printed cotton fabrics designed by William Morris during the late 1800s. A noted writer, artisan, and designer, Morris was the founding father of the Arts and Crafts movement in England and his stylized floral and nature motifs appeared on fabrics and rugs as well as wallpapers. Many of his chintz patterns were inspired by the variety of flowers native to the English countryside, and

Above: Part of the charm of English country style derives from a seemingly effortless mix of patterns in any given room. Here, a floral wallpaper blends beautifully with a variety of checkered fabrics to embellish a bedroom. A handsome sleigh-style daybed is practical as well as attractive and favorite treasures, such as a collection of dolls, make a whimsical display.

while bright colors were featured in much of his work, so, too, were the soft, muted shades that found their way into many a country home. In fact, Morris' firm decorated numerous manor houses and country estates, so there is indeed a link between the Arts and Crafts movement and English country style. Today Morris' work lives on through the fabric and wallpaper available from Arthur Sanderson & Sons Ltd. (A final word about fabrics: floral patterned chintz immediately comes to mind when we think of English country style, but don't forget that striped fabrics and checkered patterns are every bit as traditional, cheerful, and full of English charm.)

Clearly, English country style calls upon colorful printed fabrics to fashion a mellowed look, but this is just a part of its casual country appeal. Rustic English pine and oak furnishings, often scaled-down versions of period designs, filled the rooms of cottages. Pieces such as large dressers or hutches were used to store and display dishware and crockery; massive benches

Above left: A delicious cottage kitchen incorporates rustic elements: a timbered ceiling, wood cabinets and furnishings, and a practical tile floor. Blue-and-white-striped wallpaper sets the tone for a collection of blue and white plates, while floral chintz curtains, looped back, add a wonderful dose of color and English charm. *Above right:* Family heirlooms and collections on display are the essence of English country style. A paint-chipped wall with a timeworn and artistic look provides a fitting backdrop for vintage framed prints, a classical bust, and crystal candlesticks and stemware, as well as other treasured objects. *Opposite:* The owners of this inviting English country–style living room are surrounded by cherished treasures. The wall behind the comfy velvet sofa showcases a collection of gilt-framed oil paintings and prints. The carved upholstered bench used as a coffee table provides ample space for books, woodenware, and a potted plant. Even the mantel is artfully arrayed with select pottery pieces, flowers, and yet another *favorite* painting.

British Staffordshire Figures

❀ These molded and enameled decorative figures were created by several different potteries in the North Staffordshire region of England.

❀ Many different figures were created including animals, members of the royal family, and political figures. Many collectors are especially drawn to the Staffordshire spaniels, which are generally brown and white or black and white.

❀ Early examples made prior to 1840 were fully formed whereas figures produced after that date are to be seen from the front only—they feature flat backs.

❀ Lightweight forgeries are being made today, so the collector should know how to identify them.

❀ Rare examples can cost a great deal, but more common Staffordshire figures are within reach of the average collector.

provided seating in the front hall; a scrubbed-top table was at the heart of the kitchen; and a center table was piled high with books in the sitting room. Upholstered furnishings were comfortable, overstuffed, and accessorized with pillows and warm throws. Numerous side chairs and tables were scattered about for seating and space to arrange a hodgepodge of collectibles and family treasures. In contrast, the manor house had a more aristocratic air in that rooms were larger, furniture was generally of a dark wood, and there was a hint of old wealth about the place.

Above: English charm as an interpretation of country style can have a quaint cottage look or a more masculine, manor-house appeal. This wood-paneled sitting room with its leather wing chair clearly conveys the latter. A handsome medieval-style fireplace is filled with greenery when it is not being used and the mantel bears books, a mirror with an ornately carved frame, and an oil portrait. A Windsor chair provides added seating and a small table makes space for yet more books.

Collections have long been tied to the English country style. In the living room there may have been a display of miniature oil paintings in gilt frames or a charming grouping of Staffordshire figures atop the mantelpiece. Perhaps the dining room showcased a collection of lusterware or blue and white transfer-printed china. In the kitchen were pottery bowls, enameled containers, creamware, or baskets. An enormous amount of British pottery has been made over the years (going back centuries), especially in the Staffordshire region, and today collectors are drawn to slipware, which is earthenware decorated with a "slip" similar to American-made redware; salt-glazed stoneware, which can be highly decorative; cream-ware with hand-painted or transfer-print designs; Prattware, which has molded designs with hand-painted coloring; ironstone, often featuring Oriental motifs; and majolica, which was produced not only in England but in France, Italy, and the United States. British porcelain was also made in vast quantities and the wares of manufacturers such as Minton and Worcester are highly desirable and perfectly at home in an English country setting.

English country is a style that allows you to surround yourself with myriad objects that give you pleasure and bring you comfort. Relaxed ease is apparent in everything from timeworn furnishings handed down through the years to floral fabrics that invite the countryside indoors. To set the tone for this inspiring variation of country style, first look to the entryway to convey a warm and

The English Entryway

Perhaps the enduring appeal of English country style stems from the fact that it's never contrived; various furnishings, colors, and patterns happily coexist and form a harmonious, various whole. The direct opposite of minimalism,

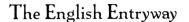

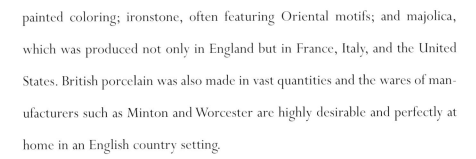

Above: This appealing cottage entryway has quintessential English charm. A country brick floor, aged plaster walls, and a front door painted blue beckon visitors inside. Wall-hung pegs make space for coats and hats, and boots can be wiped on a sisal mat. A pole lantern, riding boots, and books stacked on a table nearby add a personal decorative effect.

Floors in any entryway must be practical, and in an English country–style home where outdoor sports and gardening are intertwined with country life, floors must stand up to the rigors of boots and heavy foot traffic. Wide plank flooring with a mellow patina that's developed over time, terra-cotta tiles, flagstone, or, for a more formal manor house effect, tiles with the look of marble are all excellent choices. Add sisal matting or a sea grass floor covering or select an Oriental rug that complements your color scheme for added warmth, color, and texture. Be sure to provide a tray or special rug for footwear.

Furnishings and decorative accessories in the entryway can simply convey style, or they can convey style and the owner's interests. A tall case clock is a handsome and useful addition to the entry, as is a lovely gilt-framed mirror and an old wooden bench or settee. A table for mail, keys, packages, and the like is useful as well as decorative and can sport a table lamp for lighting and a decorative jug filled with fresh flowers. A rather nondescript table can be dressed up by using a colorful quilt as a tablecloth. Use a ceiling fixture for lighting and select a period example that has a glass globe or is fashioned to resemble a vintage lantern. Wall sconces can help brighten things up a bit, especially when they feature mini fabric shades or decorative glass globes. A row of hooks or pegs mounted on the wall is perfect for coats and hats; a Victorian-era hall tree can serve the same purpose.

To add a personal note in the entry, the avid outdoorsman or -woman might be inclined to hang hunting prints, landscape scenes, or even trophies, plaques, or taxidermy related to hunting and fishing expeditions. A lovely pottery, enameled, or wooden umbrella stand can hold walking sticks. Family portraits and photographs are yet another way to personalize this transitional space between indoors and out. A collection, whether favorite dishes arranged on a

spirited welcome. The walls in the entryway can be painted in a soft color such as sage green, apricot, old rose, or cloudy blue, with a similar or deeper shade applied to trim and woodwork. In a cottage with timber-framed walls, a stenciled design in the entryway adds a homey touch. For something more detailed, simple paneling or perhaps a subtle floral or striped wallpaper that echoes the colors of the countryside can be used.

Above: An ancestral oil portrait presides over this foyer furnished with an imposing table. A display of military medals conveys one of the owner's interests, along with a grouping of stemware and select small prints. An antique drum poised beneath the table echoes the colors in both the portrait and the military ribbons. Manor-house charm is pleasingly achieved.

wall or porcelain figurines displayed as a tabletop composition, is another decorative touch to be considered.

The English Living Room

The living room (referred to as the sitting room when discussing English country style) and dining room can reflect a simple country style or a more traditional manor house look. Architectural embellishment tends to be rather rustic, with timbered or paneled walls, wood-beamed ceilings, and perhaps almost medieval-looking leaded glass windows. A quaint fireplace is required for taking the chill off the damp night air, and a tile surround adds a cheerful decorative touch. The fireplace surround and mantel can be painted or can feature a warm wood finish.

A large-scale floral wallpaper is ideal in spacious sitting rooms and dining rooms, but a small and cozy cottage will benefit from a creamy shade of paint and perhaps just a hint of design via stenciling or a wallpaper border. Soft colors are associated with a cottage look while deeper shades, such as crimson, are well suited to the darker furnishings associated with the manor house. Special painted effects such as ragging can lend the subtle illusion of texture as well as mask imperfections in old plaster walls. In an authentic cottage with timbered walls and ceilings, exposed wood can be painted the same lovely shade as the walls or wear its natural finish.

Plank wood floors in the living room and dining room can be layered with Oriental or needlepoint rugs. Older rugs that are a bit worn but still beautiful will work best. Floors can also be covered with a room-size sisal or sea grass carpet with favorite rugs arranged over them in conversation areas or underneath the table. Wall-to-wall carpet, while not to the letter of the style, can still be charming in an English country setting, adding comfort, warmth, and a good splash of color.

Windows in the quintessential English cottage are deep-set with massive sills ideal for displays of collectibles or jugs of fresh flowers. The windows, however, tend to be small, and a simple homespun curtain or lace panel that

Above: This delightful sitting room features a brick fireplace with a wood-burning stove insert and pale, ragged walls. Sea grass carpeting is layered with a vibrant area rug that defines space and repeats the blue and red color scheme. Simple but attractive drapes with a lace-edged valance contribute cottage charm, as do an assortment of fresh flowers and plump chair pillows.

Above left: *A deep-set window, typical of many English country homes, allows plenty of space for an inviting window seat and a display of favorite objects. Sunlight streams through unadorned windows and beckons you to linger for an hour or two with a good book. A bouquet of fresh flowers in an attractive jug is a signature mark of an English country decorating style.*

Above right: *A soft and pale green fireplace wall includes an old wood-beam mantel with evocative traces of faded paint. A low, timbered ceiling, chintz-covered sofa, and plush white easy chair capture the essence of English country style. A rustic wood coffee table sports a lovely piece of pottery that echoes the cobalt blue in the pottery-based lamp. A willow basket holds wood for the fireplace while floral bouquets and select ceramic pieces atop the mantel convey old-fashioned country taste.*

can be tied back to allow precious light in is a popular treatment. Plain cotton, striped ticking, and a subtle chintz are the fabrics of choice, and curtain rods of wood or iron with decorative finials are suitable. In many cases an attractive valance is all that's called for at a tiny window. In contrast, large windows are made lovely when dressed with floor-length drapes that are looped back with decorative cords. Austrian shades, swags, and valances can also be used in a more romantic or traditional setting.

While less can be more, when it comes to the English country–style living room, it's definitely the more the merrier. Every nook and cranny is filled with tables and chairs—more traditional styles in the manor house setting and simple but sturdy handcrafted pieces for the cottage. Windsor chairs and ladder-back chairs with cushioned rush seats accompany a plump, overstuffed sofa and easy chairs that are the epitome of country comfort. Fabrics tend to be practical but also decorative and include cotton chintz, striped ticking, wool, and linen. Checkered patterns are also at home here and are sometimes combined with a floral chintz for a vibrant play of color and pattern. Loose-fitting slipcovers are appealing in the cottage, while fitted upholstery with a tailored skirt or leather seating is associated with the more upscale manor house look. One word of caution, however, in regard to chintz: don't overdecorate with it. Rather, use chintz sparingly to enhance, not dominate, the room.

While darker woods such as mahogany are associated with the manor house, honey pine is de rigueur in the cottage. If there is any one piece that stands as a symbol of the English country style, it would have to be the large dresser—a cupboard with open shelving on top and cupboard doors down below that proves ideal for both display and storage. And the English dresser can be used in the sitting room and dining room as well as the homey country

The Elements of English Country Style

* Timbered walls and ceilings, leaded glass windows, and small fireplaces
* Chintz fabric as well as gingham, stripes, checks, and lace
* Scrubbed pine, oak, and mahogany furnishings
* Wallpapers with William Morris designs, floral chintz patterns, and stripes
* Decorative accessories such as hunting and fishing gear and memorabilia, family portraits and photos, books, flowers, travel souvenirs, and baskets
* Collectibles such as china, pottery, colored glass bottles and jars, and enamelware

sitting room very cozy, and the fireplace can become a focal point when decorating with a vintage or reproduction tile surround. In a cottage setting, wildflowers, baskets, quilted pillows and table covers, warm throws, books, family photos, assorted collectibles, and pottery, glass, or brass candlesticks will convey the spirit of English charm. The manor house tends to be a bit more refined, with travel souvenirs, needlepoint pillows, and porcelain on display.

The English Dining Room

The background in the dining room is designed in much the same way as in the sitting room. Choose wallpaper, paint, or paneling for walls and consider adding a special touch such as a chair rail or a dado/field wallpaper effect in a more traditional setting. A William Morris wallpaper with a stylized floral pattern is very effective used in tandem with wood paneling or a corresponding shade of paint. Colors associated with the dining room tend to be a bit deeper, such as forest green, medium blue, and darker variations of red. Add an Oriental or needlepoint rug that blends with your color scheme.

Dining room furnishings in the English country–style home can be crafted of handsome dark woods such as mahogany or oak that's been treated to a rich stain. Nineteenth-century period furnishings are called for in a manor house setting—large rectangular tables and chairs with tapestry upholstered seats. Simpler pieces that don't necessarily match will suit the cottage look just fine.

kitchen. Other well-crafted furnishings are often painted in soft colors and sometimes decorated with hand-painted floral motifs or a romantic stenciled design. Hanging cupboards for small trinkets, a trunk used as a coffee table, and even assorted tables and chairs can be treated to a transforming coat of paint.

Use table lamps with attractive pottery bases and pleated fabric shades for lighting or a more traditional candlestick or urn-shaped lamp with a linen shade. Wall sconces and a floor lamp are wonderful additions, providing ambiance as well as task or localized lighting. Candlelight and firelight make the

Above: Pastel painted walls, a timbered ceiling, and a wood floor make pleasing surroundings for a medley of furnishings and accessories in this dining room. The light wood table and chairs contrast quite nicely with the hewn timber mantel and dark, paneled door. A colorful, upholstered chair, an eye-catching mantel display, fresh flowers, and a pottery collection make this an enchanting place for family meals.

For example, a plain round table can be covered with a vintage quilt, floor-length colorful fabric, or a lace tablecloth. A warm pine table with a medley of chairs or painted furniture can also be used in the cozy dining room. Accessorize chairs with chintz, gingham, or striped cushions for added comfort.

Above: A long, rectangular pine table allows plenty of room for family and friends in this handsome dining room. By adding a substantial china cupboard and a sideboard of rich, dark woods, there's plenty of space for pottery, dishware, and collectibles. Elegant floral displays, an antique chandelier, and select artwork enhance the room's intimate elegance.

Additional furniture pieces in the dining room might include a pine or oak dresser for storing dishware, linens, and cutlery. A beautiful pine armoire is also ideal for linens, or a notable mahogany sideboard. The charms peculiar to this English country style are most definitely found in the subtle blending of furniture (with various degrees of ornamentation) that spans a great number of years—the period styles as well as the home-crafted, utilitarian pieces. This medley is always comfortable and inviting.

Decorative accessories in the dining room include an array of items from antique lighting fixtures (perhaps a chandelier and wall sconces) and a gilt-framed mirror to curtains or draperies appropriate to the level of the room's decor. A traditional setting calls for slightly elegant drapes, perhaps of damask, while lace or chintz will do nicely in a more casual setting. Family portraits, traditional candlesticks, and a collection of dishware will make the room complete.

The English Bedroom

The bedroom in the English country–style home can pay tribute to past centuries by blending various furnishings, decorative touches, and window treatments together to fashion a romantic, appealing hideaway. Walls may be painted in a pastel hue and perhaps embellished with a floral, leaf, or trailing ivy design. Then again, a lovely wallpaper with a mini print design or a small floral pattern is perfect for the style. Wallpaper also works wonders in unifying the small under-the-eaves spaces so common in the cottage house.

Plank wood floors in the bedroom can be painted and even stenciled or softened with a decorative area rug. Floors can also be covered with a room-size sisal or sea grass matting with smaller area rugs as accents. Wall-to-wall carpet in a sumptuous shade of color can be used to anchor the room.

Above: This cozy sitting area in an under-the-eaves cottage bedroom features a successful medley of diverse furniture pieces. An ornate mirror contributes an elegant touch of formality while a checker-pattern wing chair salutes country style. A small pine trunk spotlights a jug of fresh flowers and a chest has been embellished with a hand-painted floral design. Such a mix never looks contrived—just natural. *Opposite:* A sloped, timbered ceiling adds dramatic flair in this English country bedroom and creates an abundance of space for a stunning canopy bed. An old-fashioned quilt and needlepoint pillows make the bed complete. Manor-house charm is also conveyed by adding several small rugs and select personal accessories.

Windows may be large or small but the emphasis is on creating a treatment that's as lovely as it is functional. Depending upon whether your English country bedroom tends to be traditional or more in a cottage style, floor-length chintz draperies or perhaps lace curtains with a pretty print valance may be desired. Austrian shades or attractive fabric or wood blinds can also be used, as well as some combination of the above, such as print draperies tied back and sporting a matching valance, perhaps with a lacy edge. And while small floral designs immediately come to mind when considering the bedroom, a cheerful gingham

or striped window dressing is every bit as appealing and appropriate to the style. Keep in mind that while you don't necessarily want to create a "decorated" look, the window dressing can be selected to coordinate with the bedcover or an upholstery fabric. Restraint is obviously key.

Furnishings in the bedroom, though not matching suites, should blend effortlessly together. The bedroom reminiscent of the English manor house may include a beautiful four-poster canopy bed or a half-tester (half-canopy) bed. In such a case a luxurious chintz can be used for bed curtains. In contrast, a favorite

Above left: This attic bedroom retreat displays a wonderful mix of playful colors and textures. An exposed timber ceiling endows the room with cottage ambiance and the wall behind the bed, the color of spun gold, incorporates a decorative stencil design. Shelves tucked into corners are painted in blues and greens while a simple low-poster bed with a patchwork quilt becomes the obvious center of attention.

Above right: Traditional English country style is achieved in this handsome bedroom by blending sleek, dark wood furnishings with a rich, floral pattern. The same fabric is used for the window dressing, bedspread, canopy, and padded bench at the foot of the bed—combined with the massive architectural bed posts, this results in elegant manor-house appeal. A Windsor armchair, bedside table, and framed prints provide additional comforts of home.

in the more casual cottage-style bedroom is an old iron bedstead embellished with metal trimwork and decorative curlicues. Painted black, white, or maybe dark green, a metal bed can be eye-catching when accessorized with an heirloom quilt or a dust ruffle and chintz spread. Painted furniture is also quite popular; a headboard decorated in a soft creamy shade can become a striking focal point with hand-painted floral designs. A fabric-padded headboard will work in either setting and can be quite inviting when bedecked with a matching bedskirt, a warm comforter or throw, and several plump pillows.

Other furnishings in the bedroom, including dressers, a dressing table, perhaps a desk and chair, and a vintage marbletop or tiled washstand, might be period pieces or the handiwork of country craftsmen. They may wear a gleaming wood finish or coat of paint and a delightful decorative design. An overstuffed easy chair and ottoman may be present for lounging, and the preferred choice for a bedside table is a round table (or two) covered with a generous tablecloth that has just a hint of ruffled trim. Decorative pottery lamps can then provide light for bedtime reading, and favorite books can be stacked nearby. As always, to complete the setting, add a fresh bouquet of flowers, cherished objects on display, botanical prints on the wall—then go ahead and relax in the soothing country comfort you've created.

The English Kitchen

The English country–style kitchen and bathroom retain their old-world charm while at the same time meeting modern-day needs in an unobtrusive way. A low timbered ceiling in the kitchen creates a cozy atmosphere, and as the heart of the country home, this space calls upon age-old materials and the spirit of timelessness to contribute to its sense of style. First, old plaster walls or more

modern plasterboard is color-washed or painted in a subtle shade such as creamy yellow, pink, terra-cotta, or light green. Ragging can add heightened visual interest. Brick and tile also lend themselves as wall treatments,

Above: A simple provincial feeling helps define this charming cottage kitchen. Old plaster walls are painted white and accented with a tongue-and-groove pine ceiling. A muted, pale green paint has been used on the kitchen door and plank storage cabinet. A vintage, cream-colored enameled stove is practical as well as comforting. By adding select items, such as the large basket, a framed map, and a primitive stool, this quaint kitchen exudes old-world country style.

a rustic look about it, you'll want a flooring treatment that's composed of or resembles a natural material.

To outfit the country kitchen for style as well as practical ease, consider built-in cupboards (bottom or lower cupboards) with a honey pine finish or a creamy shade of paint. Architectural embellishment should be kept to a minimum, just simple moldings and porcelain or brass pulls. Top base cabinets off with a tile, wood, or marble countertop, and rather than hanging top cupboards, opt instead for open shelving to store dishware.

No English country kitchen would be complete without a large dresser or hutch with glass-front cupboard doors to display china and pottery. Equally important is a scrubbed-top table in the kitchen for family meals. The table can be outfitted with a mix of chairs and cushions used for comfort and decoration. Last but not least, the venerable Aga stove, which has been a fixture in English kitchens for ages, is large with several ovens and an attractive porcelain enamel finish.

Decorative accessories in the kitchen include old-fashioned (whether antique or reproduction) lighting fixtures, collections on display, and spirited chintz, gingham, or striped window dressings. Fill the English dresser with odd pieces of china, majolica, ironstone pottery, a collection of teapots, or blue and white dishware. Copper cookware can be hung from a rack; herbs

especially behind the stove or around the fireplace. Decorative tile is also used as a backsplash in counter areas. Wallpaper is another option provided it's a scrubbable vinyl paper. Look at country-style mini prints such as a Laura Ashley wallpaper (see Sources) or select a striped or floral pattern.

Floors of wood, brick, terra-cotta tiles, or modern-day resilient flooring with the look of brick or tile are preferred. Place rag rugs or small needlepoint rugs in work stations for comfort. Since the English country–style kitchen has

Above: This spacious kitchen conveys English charm through its cream-colored walls and cabinets, plank flooring, a tile backsplash in blue and white checks, and a venerable Aga stove. A large round table for family meals sports a blue-and-white-checkered cloth, and the same color scheme and pattern are repeated in select pottery pieces. An overhead rack proves ideal for drying linens and clothing near the warmth of the stove, while a beautiful bank of windows and striking door bring garden views indoors.

Opposite: Natural elements such as a tile floor, wooden countertop, and beautiful pine pieces infuse this setting with English country style. Cabinets and a wood wainscoting in the breakfast nook have been painted a lovely blue-green shade. A honey-colored pine table, chairs, and a cushioned settee provide the perfect spot for casual meals. A pine glass-front hanging cupboard displays blue and white china while cookbooks and decorative accessories such as flowers, fruit, and colorful window valances, contribute perfect finishing touches.

enamelware made during the same period, English examples are charmingly simple with little in the way of ornamentation except for plain stenciled or raised lettering to denote the contents of sundry containers.

The English Bathroom

In the English country–style bath, the influence of the Victorian age is strongly felt. An old-fashioned claw-foot tub and pedestal sink can be accompanied by a tile floor with a traditional diamond pattern. An elegant bath can be created by encasing the tub in dark wood paneling and then fashioning a vanity from a vintage sideboard or washstand. Brass hardware adds a certain

and flowers can be placed in clay pots on a window ledge; and baskets used for fruits and vegetables, and collectible enamelware, such as canisters and a bread box, can enliven a shelf or countertop.

Vintage British enamelware, those pieces produced between the late 1800s and 1940, were turned out in white and pale shades such as yellow, baby blue, and light green. Unlike much of the decorated French and other European

ambiance, as do old-fashioned lighting fixtures and a well-loved Oriental rug.

Wallpaper, decorative tiles, or both are found here—on walls, as a backsplash behind the sink, or as a tub surround. And creature comforts are close by—thick, warm towels and a collection of toiletries and grooming necessities. The bath calls for a gilt-framed mirror, lush plants, perhaps a collection of colored glass bottles, and an old china water jug and basin. Even in the tiny cottage, the bath is treated as a room and not just a utilitarian space. Every need is met, comfort is provided for, and the level of decoration rivals that of any other room in the English country-style home, if in an understated key.

Above: *A large pine or painted kitchen dresser filled to overflowing is a hallmark of English country style. Providing ample space for display, these dresser shelves show off an assortment of blue and white china, yellowware, and traditional butter molds.*

Left: A more formal approach has been taken in outfitting this handsome bath. Rich wood cabinetry provides storage space on either side of the pedestal sink and the tub has been encased in a similar fashion. Walls have been treated to a dado / field effect by using moldings to define space, and the upper portion of the bathroom wall combines a decorative paint with a subtle stencil design. An area rug and antique chair provide added comfort while an eye-catching mirror and crisp, metal towel rack are both attractive and practical. Flowers, toiletries, and artwork embellish this relaxing retreat.

Right: Just as charming and decorative as any other room in the house, this cottage bath with timbered walls makes full use of blue and white tiles to fashion a tub surround. An old-style pedestal sink pays tribute to the past, as does the lovely cane-back chair and Oriental area rug. A simple blue-and-white-striped curtain repeats the color scheme and matches the country-style chair cushion. Note, too, the witty wallscape created with a collection of cheerful plates. A bouquet of roses and porcelain figurines add to the room's appealing character.

Chapter Seven

American Farmhouse

America's heartland and rural back roads all across the nation are dotted with farmhouses, many of which have stood the test of time. In days past these country homes were outfitted for utility as well as homey comfort, and today this appealing farmhouse style has moved to the fore-front of the country decorating craze.

Living and working in remote areas during the late nine-teenth and early twentieth centuries meant that a trip to a far-away town or city was a grand adventure indeed. The farmer's wife might make a list of necessities she needed to buy, but more often than not she relied on the mail-order catalogue to purchase goods for the home and the family. She could shop from the comfort of her kitchen table and still have the benefit of afford-able, stylish furnishings, fabrics, and household goods. Not that the farmhouse was the epitome of the latest style—it had an almost spartan but comfortable, lived-in look. Frivolous items were uncalled for and hard-earned cash was spent on practical items: sturdy furniture, ser-viceable cotton fabrics, and household necessities such as kitchenware for cooking, baking, or putting up preserves.

Above: Old Glory is front and center in this American farmhouse-style setting. Scaled-back furnishings and decorative accessories can have big impact in this pop-ular interpretation of country style. As seen here, a Neoclassical desk—perhaps a family heirloom—is dressed with a patriotic theme and positioned against a floral wallpapered wall. A graceful swag at the window adds elegance. Opposite: This perfect farmhouse kitchen features wallpaper with a fruit motif appropriate to the homey setting. A small but decorative screen, also dressed with a fruit design, becomes a charming focal point. Furnishings include a pine cabinet, ideal for storage and display, that blends effortlessly with the pine wainscoting and kitchen trim. A scrubbed-top table provides a spot for casual meals, while select accessories, such as yellowware, a jug of flowers, and a birdcage suspended from a wood beam, imbue this room with spirit.

Decorative items were called for but they were not costly, and many pieces were handmade at home. For example, while a family may have bought a lovely gilt-trimmed service for the dining room table (which was cherished and well cared for), scraps of material were recycled into quilts and braided rugs. Purchases were well thought out and absolutely nothing was wasted.

The humble origins, appealing simplicity, and warm, homespun character of the farmhouse had all the makings of a distinct style by the late 1800s. Painted cupboards, chairs, and benches as well as utilitarian items such as the kitchen dry sink, baker's cupboard, and later the Hoosier cabinet were combined with mostly oak furnishings. And while the painted pieces may have been homemade or at least in the family for years, the oak furnishings were almost a novelty in that they could easily be obtained from the Sears, Roebuck & Company or Montgomery Ward & Company catalogues that catered to the large rural population. A sampling of the departments included in the 1895 Montgomery Ward catalogue shows that farm families could order everything from clothing, sewing notions, and toiletries to wallpaper, carpets, curtains, and furniture.

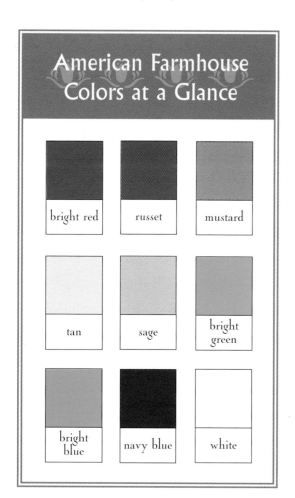

American Farmhouse Colors at a Glance

bright red	russet	mustard
tan	sage	bright green
bright blue	navy blue	white

Farmhouse Interior Treatments

The wallpapers available via mail order during the late 1890s were offered in colors such as red, tan, pearl, gray, olive, ecru, pale blue, pink, cream, and terra-cotta. Patterns included floral sprays, geometric designs, stripes, leaves, scrolls, flower buds, and floral wreaths. Gilt-trimmed wallpapers were advertised as being highly popular for the parlor and dining room, but these may

Above: Simple homespun character is conveyed via this kitchen sink encased in an American farmhouse cabinet reminiscent of an antique dry sink. Made with pine bead board, and providing space to hang kitchen collectibles, it's the very essence of country spirit. By adding a striking braided rug fashioned to follow the curves of this handsome piece, this country setting is complete.

have been a bit too extravagant for the farmhouse. Plain and simple was better. Costwise, catalogue readers were told they could paper an entire room for well under a dollar, making wallpaper a popular decorative option. Decorative moldings, chair rails, and even wallpaper borders were available to spruce up any room in the house.

The store-bought carpets and rugs that made their way into the farmhouse usually sported floral designs and were used along with hooked rugs and braided rugs for warmth and comfort more than for show. Ingrain carpets, hemp carpets, and Brussels carpets were among the more popular options, with ingrains thought to be the most practical since they were reversible. Hemp carpets, many of which featured colorful striped designs, were recommended for high-traffic areas such as hallways. Oilcloth in decorative patterns was also available through catalogues for the farmhouse kitchen floor.

Lace curtains and window shades could be ordered through a catalogue in the late nineteenth century and were especially delightful in the farmhouse where open spaces meant soft summer breezes blowing through open windows. For the women who preferred to make their own curtains, the fabrics available included white dotted Swiss muslin, plain white organdy, and point d'esprit, which was advertised in one catalogue as "a white lace net of small mesh with tiny worked spots scattered profusely over it." The dotted Swiss curtain remains an especially appealing window treatment in today's farmhouse decorating style.

Above: Simple is lovely in this American farmhouse–style bedroom, where windows have been dressed in sheer ruffled curtains that are casually looped back for country appeal. Floral wallpaper creates an ideal backdrop for a substantial bed sporting a cozy comforter. A wicker planter and small rocker are charming additions and provide subtle, decorative contrast to the plain pine plank floor.

Farmhouse Furniture

Oak furniture could be found in any and every room in the turn-of-the-century farmhouse. The Industrial Revolution of the nineteenth century made it possible for factories, many of which were located in Grand Rapids, Michigan, to turn out large quantities of oak or oak-look-alike (made of elm, ash, or chestnut) furnishings. Much of this furniture was treated to a clear varnish that gave it a golden appearance, and machinery was available to create stamped or steam-pressed decorative designs such as those found on pressed-back chairs.

The wide selection of oak furnishings available through the mail-order catalogue was impressive. For the kitchen there were oak iceboxes, tables, and chairs plus a freestanding cupboard for dishware. For the bedroom there were matching chamber suites that included a bed, a chest of drawers, and a washstand or commode. Three-piece suites for the living room (starting at around $14 in the late 1890s) included a sofa, an armchair, and a rocker; a five-piece grouping with an additional two chairs could also be bought. Cotton tapestry was a popular upholstery fabric, or a silk plush or brocatelle could be ordered. Some sets were quite basic and serviceable while others were ornamented with detailed carvings and upholstery trim. Other furniture available included dining room suites, bookcases, parlor tables, library tables, wardrobes, hall trees, mirrors, hat racks, assorted chairs, child-size pieces, and rocking chairs.

The rocking chair, in fact, was an important part of the farmhouse decor. A rocker was often found in the kitchen near the warmth of the wood stove, in the parlor, and on the front porch. Rural Americans were quite taken with the rocking chair, which was no doubt the reason why the 1900 Sears, Roebuck & Company catalogue included several different oak models, many of which were advertised as "broad and roomy." They could be ordered with a leather, wood, or upholstered seat and were priced anywhere from $1.45 to $4.75, the latter for an elegant example with fancy carvings, turned spindles, and a leather seat.

The living room in the farmhouse usually had a fireplace for warmth on cold winter evenings and the mantel was of a simple design in oak or painted wood. Atop the mantel could be found the parlor clock, and while ornate, marbleized, or enameled iron examples were available, in the farmhouse the mantel clock was more likely to have a case of polished oak or walnut. Naturally clocks could be purchased through the mail-order catalogue.

Other necessities and decorative items in the farmhouse included family photographs, oil lamps, inexpensive prints in pretty gilt frames, framed hand-stitched mottoes such as "Bless Our Home," baskets, quilts, samplers, colored glassware, pottery bowls, and graniteware.

The American farmhouse interpretation of country style can easily be created in today's country home even if the house is not in a rural setting. Apartments and suburban ranches can have a farmhouse feel with simple and colorful backgrounds, carefully selected furnishings, and decorative accessories limited to a few a chosen favorites. American farmhouse is a style balanced somewhere between the austere beauty of Shaker simplicity and the cluttered, romantic appeal of country Victorian style.

Opposite: This modern take on American farmhouse style calls upon favorite country colors—red, white, and blue—to fashion an inviting living room. With the hearth as a focal point, this setting is furnished with a rocking chair (the quintessential farmhouse piece), a wing chair upholstered in red and blue, a deep blue sofa, and a vintage trunk given new life as a coffee table. Grouped baskets and candlesticks create collections on display while a hand-hooked rug claims a place of honor above the hearth.

Above left: This pared-down decorating scheme in an American farmhouse entryway conveys a hearty autumn welcome. Simple touches such as a pumpkin beside the entrance and Indian corn hung on the door are small touches that say a great deal. Indoors, aged, chip-painted walls and a rugged plank floor create a lived-in country ambiance. A single chair, sporting a straw hat, completes the "less is more" approach to decorating this inviting space.

Above right: This spirited farmhouse entryway features a bold plank wall, painted red, and a crisp white ceiling. Wide plank flooring is accented with a homey rag rug, and select accessories, such as the stoneware crock with a cobalt blue design and a framed painting, add the perfect measure of country spirit. A traditional painted jelly cupboard is perfect in the entry, since it is useful for storage and allows space for small keepsakes.

The Farmhouse Entryway

To begin, many houses feature an inviting front porch; if your home does indeed have one, a few painted rocking chairs will set a cheerful and welcoming tone. Beyond the front door (which might include a seasonal wreath or a lovely art-glass or etched glass window), the entryway can be decorated in old-fashioned farmhouse style by painting walls a lively, warm shade, such as red, or a more subdued green or blue. If neutral colors or muted shades are more to your liking, tan, khaki, or terra-cotta might be preferred. Woodwork can be left with a natural wood finish or updated with a coat of white paint.

The floor in the farmhouse entry can be hardwood, wide planks, or an eye-catching colored or checkered tile. Add a rag rug, braided rug, or floral hooked rug. Vintage rugs can be found at antiques shops and shows, but with the renewed interest in folk art and homey crafts, kits for making your own rugs are also available in a wide array of patterns and designs.

Furnishings and decorative accessories in the entryway should be limited to what's practical, keeping in mind that practical can also be beautiful: an oak hall tree for coats and hats, a mirrored coat rack with hooks or a simple row of pegs, an oak or painted chair for putting on boots, and perhaps a small oak table or painted bench for dropping mail. An overhead lighting fixture, such as an iron or brass example with a glass shade, will prove handy, and a framed print or soft pastel will make a nice addition to a wall.

The Farmhouse Living Room

The living room and dining room in the country farmhouse setting are warm, inviting, and surprisingly lively. These rooms have clean lines and an uncluttered look, with a casual treatment designed to put select furnishings center

stage. Paint walls a bright, creamy yellow, pale sage green, off-white, pearl gray, or soft blue. Actually, your choices in regard to color are far from limited, so select your favorite shade provided that it's not too deep or dark. Remember, the American farmhouse style is light and airy. In regard to trim, a wood finish has a certain authentic appeal, but you can't go wrong with a coat of white paint.

For those who prefer wallpaper, the farmhouse-style living room and dining room can be decorated with a paper that has a white, cream, or

Above: A blue and white color scheme is ideal in the American farmhouse-style living room. Here, architectural embellishments such as ceiling beams and the decorative fireplace wall have been painted a lovely shade of blue. An uncluttered approach to furnishings keeps the space light and airy. An Oriental area rug contributes a sophisticated accent, while windows are dressed with floral-patterned curtains that are casually tied back.

neutral-colored background and a small yet colorful floral, geometric, or scroll design. Striped wallpaper is also a popular option in a casual country farmhouse setting.

A lovely oak hardwood or wide plank floor (which has a more rustic look) can be used in the dining or living room and accented with colorful rag rugs or a floral hooked rug. If underneath that wall-to-wall carpeting you have hardwood floors, you might want to consider removing the carpet to expose the beauty of the wood and heighten the appeal of your farmhouse-style home. If, on the other hand, you love the comfort of carpet or are not able to remove it, you can still layer area rugs to impart a sense of country style.

Above: Oftentimes, especially in a rural or very private setting, a scenic view may be preferred to a window treatment. When possible, by all means allow the outdoors inside by treating a window as a decorative element in its own right. A generous ledge can become a display shelf of sorts, playing host to a lovely bowl of fruit.

Windows in a country farmhouse decorating scheme are loveliest when plain and serene. Dotted Swiss, muslin, and linen tab curtains are all excellent choices, and lace panels can also be used to create a light and airy country-style window treatment. Tailored curtains without ruffles, fancy valances, or trim are preferred, and while white or natural-colored fabrics can be used with any color scheme, you may prefer a window treatment with a dash of color that blends nicely with walls or upholstery. It's simply a matter of personal choice. And don't forget handsome wood, brass, or iron curtain rods, which can be as lovely and decorative as the curtains. Then again, in a rural or very private setting, you may decide that no window dressing is the best dressing of all.

Furnishings and decorative accessories in the country farmhouse setting should be comfortable and practical. The farmhouse of a century ago may have featured a Victorian parlor suite (proper but certainly short on comfort), but today's home calls for something much more welcoming. A large tailored sofa with a checkered, striped, or petite floral pattern or solid-colored upholstery can be paired with a cozy easy chair or perhaps a matching love seat. Add a vintage or reproduction oak rocking chair to inject farmhouse flavor along with oak parlor tables and an old-fashioned trunk or a painted bench to serve as a put-your-feet-up coffee table. An oak bookcase, a painted step-back cupboard, and plant stands can also be added provided that the room doesn't begin to take on a crowded or cluttered look.

For lighting, kerosene lamps wired for electricity have an old-fashioned farmhouse charm; you can also choose stoneware, pottery, or iron lamps with winsome fabric shades. Fabric lamp shades in a checkered or striped pattern or a small mini print can add visual interest. And speaking of fabric, keep a vintage quilt or two nearby for curling up on the sofa and remember that throw

Above: A bright patterned wallpaper, plank flooring, and white trim create the perfect frame for this farmhouse-style living room. A blue area rug adds warmth and a good dose of color, echoing the blue in the upholstered wing chair. Two rocking chairs add homey comfort and country charm. Collections are obviously an important part of the room's decor, from the various bells hanging from the wood beam and iron utensils next to the old-fashioned open hearth to the assorted treasures atop the simple horizontal of the mantel.

pillows can be crafted from recycled quilt scraps. A basket full of logs for the fireplace, a jug filled with fresh flowers, and family photos in attractive frames all contribute to the homey atmosphere.

Walls in the living room can play host to your favorite artwork but you don't want to overdo it. A lovely framed print, a pastel landscape scene, or an evocative watercolor would be a nice addition. To recall the past, you might want to hang a collection of framed samplers. Handsome wood or gilt frames will set off artwork quite nicely.

Above left: Soft green walls and a vintage piano updated with a similar shade of paint make a pleasing combination in this country-style living room. The window has been treated to simple pine moldings and a shade that can be pulled for privacy. A kerosene lamp and a small table displaying seashells gives the setting a subtle personal touch.

Above right: A striking stenciled border sets off the simple half-paneling on the wall of this appealing room. A drop-leaf table holds an antique pitcher that has been given new life as a vase, and a folk art painting of a cow adds a truly rustic touch.

Finally, avoid clutter on tabletops: keep collectibles to a minimum and allow room for your favorite books, magazines, and a candlestick or two. A mantel clock, a treasured piece of folk art, or colored glass pitchers or jugs make a wonderful manteltop display.

The Farmhouse Dining Room

For the dining room, seek out an antique or reproduction oak table and pressed-back chairs. Tables can be round or rectangular, and chairs are available in a variety of styles with either cane or wooden seats and various levels of ornamentation. Fortunately, such an abundance of oak furniture was made between the late 1800s and the early years of the twentieth century that it's still possible to find nice pieces at affordable prices. Also be on the lookout for an oak sideboard or china cabinet, either of which would be an apt addition to the farmhouse-inspired dining room. Equally at home in the farmhouse-style dining room is a long harvest table accompanied by Windsor or ladder-back chairs. Long benches can even be used if outfitted with plump, comfy cushions. Team a harvest table with a painted cupboard for a more rustic air and take advantage of the shelf space by displaying a collection of vintage dishware.

Decorative accessories in the farmhouse dining room include a metal chandelier with curved arms or a more decorative hanging fixture with a hand-painted glass or colorful fabric shade. A dimmer switch is always a good idea so that you can control the level of lighting above the dining room table. Decorative wall sconces are always a nice addition in the dining room. For other decorative touches, cover the dining room table with a colorful quilt or linen

tablecloth. A favorite quilt can also be carefully hung on the wall to serve as a country-style focal point; attach it to a covered board and be sure it's not in direct sunlight. A wooden bowl or stoneware crock filled with geraniums makes a nice centerpiece. And table settings in the farmhouse-style dining room can be striking: set the table with white ironstone china or a delicate china with floral buds or sprays. Pull out the heirloom Limoges for special occasions along with the colored stemware.

Above: Discreet elegance is the key to this American farmhouse dining room. Creamy walls, a classical table and upholstered chairs, a mantel case clock, and an Oriental rug all add a traditional air. Windows are outfitted with handsome shutters that act as architectural embellishments. The table is set for tea with a beautiful linen and lace tablecloth and a simple bouquet of flowers. Simplicity, a hallmark of the American farmhouse style, can indeed be beautiful.

One last thought: what about carved or metalwork barnyard animals in the dining room? During the 1970s and early 1980s, country-style homes often featured an overabundance of cows, roosters, hens, pigs, and other animals in every conceivable configuration, shape, and form. Today's country decorating, especially the American farmhouse interpretation of the style, allows for the whimsical addition of an animal or two—especially in folk art or metalwork form—but keep in mind that excess will lead to kitsch.

The Farmhouse Bedroom

If there's any room in the farmhouse where you might indulge just a bit of excess, it has to be the bedroom. Walls can be painted in a soft and cool restful shade (such as green or blue) or white for a crisp, clean look. Wallpaper always works well in the bedroom; a mini print, stripes, or a small floral pattern would be ideal. Antique or quality handcrafted patchwork quilts can often inspire the color scheme in the farmhouse country bedroom. Favorite old-

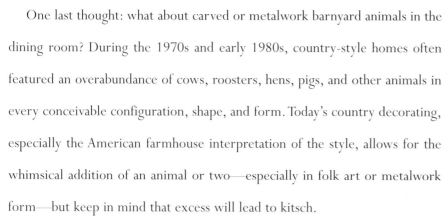

Above: An antique or reproduction cupboard in the dining room is ideal for showcasing a favorite collection and conveying the American farmhouse interpretation of country style. Here, a pine corner cupboard, resting against a homey wallpapered backdrop, includes a whimsical display of hens and select dishware.

Above: This casual dining area off the kitchen evokes the American farmhouse spirit by blending together various elements of the style. A round table and vintage chairs (sporting red and white braided chair pads) join an antique cupboard that's ideal for displaying colored glass pitchers lined up in a row. The cupboard also presents a simple yellowware bowl filled with fruit and a folk-art rooster. A colorful striped rug defines space and reinforces the red, white, and blue color scheme.

fashioned quilt patterns include the many variations of the log cabin design, the double wedding ring, the Dresden plate, and Grandmother's flower garden. Each is quite special and lovely and would make a colorful focal point in the country-inspired bedroom.

Floors in the bedroom are typically surfaced with wood, either narrow hardwood strips or wide plank boards. Oftentimes a plank floor in the bedroom is painted and might be given a decorative effect such as spattering with flecks of colored paint. Add a room-size or area braided, rag, or hooked rug for warmth and comfort. Bedrooms with wall-to-wall carpeting should feature a pale or neutral color to blend into the background, so that the bedstead, and other furnishings and decorative accessories can take center stage. A room-size sisal mat or carpet can also be introduced for country flair, then layered with casual scatter rugs for a softer touch.

Windows in the farmhouse country bedroom can be dressed in a simple tab or tailored curtain or something a bit more dressy, such as ruffled curtains pulled back at the sides. A crescent valance or swag can always be used in tandem with a roll-up shade for a lighter look. White or natural muslin, linen, or lace is best, but a bit of color such as a striped, checkered, or floral fabric can be color-coordinated to comfortably match your decorating scheme.

Furnishings and decorative accessories in the farmhouse-inspired bedroom can vary. Since this interpretation of country crosses a spectrum of periods and styles, the bed (the focal point of any bedroom) may be a handsome four-

poster, a simple low-post bed, an oak bed from the late 1800s, or an iron bedstead. Even a rustic- or primitive-looking painted bed can be striking in an American farmhouse-style bedroom.

Mix or match other furnishings as you see fit. For example, a full turn-of-the-century oak bedroom suite with a bed, chest of drawers, and washstand will clearly convey casual country style, but so too will an iron bed accompa-

Above: Farmhouse country comfort and appeal is obvious in this inviting bedroom. Flowered wallpaper has been chosen to adorn the walls, and simple bouquets continue the floral theme. A sheer, ruffled curtain and a white bedspread and canopy make the most of the room's limited natural light. The rich, dark wood of the four-poster bed is echoed in the dresser and framed mirror, and in the beautiful antique cradle.

nied by a lovely old pine dresser. A vintage steamer trunk, a small oak table, or a colorful painted bench or chair can serve as a bedside stand. An antique wardrobe can be ideal if you're short on closet space, or it can be customized to hide a small television behind closed doors. Naturally you'll want to add a

The Elements of American Farmhouse Style

❀ Chip-painted furnishings, oak furnishings, and upholstered pieces with striped, checkered, and mini-print fabrics

❀ Lace, linen, and muslin tailored or tab curtains

❀ Decorative items such as hooked or braided rugs, flowers, herbs, old prints in gilt frames, and family photos

❀ Collectibles such as stoneware, baskets, folk art, samplers, and graniteware

comfortable chair to relax in—perhaps something with striped ticking, a crewelwork pattern, or a tapestry design. And there's always room for that treasured family heirloom—the painted blanket box, Grandfather's old oak desk, or a child-size painted cupboard.

Dress the bed for solid comfort. Patchwork quilts are a natural choice for the American farmhouse bedroom. Beautiful vintage quilts can still be found in antique stores, or you can select a modern quilt made in a traditional pattern. You can also make use of a colorful goose-down comforter or a delicate embroidered spread. Sometimes a striking plaid blanket is all that's called for in a scaled-down setting. Use a bed skirt as an added decorative effect; in the farmhouse-inspired bedroom, a ruffled rather than tailored example will be more in keeping with the spirit of the style.

Make the bedroom a homey retreat with a cozy bedside lamp and a stack of favorite books, a comfortable throw, and keepsakes such as family photos. Add a basket of flowers or hang a floral wreath on the wall. Perhaps you have a collection of handmade dolls you can display on a shelf or a collection of quilts that can be folded and stacked in a small, open cupboard. Surround yourself with those quaint relics of the past that bring you a sense of comfort and appreciation for days gone by.

Opposite: A coordinated look was successfully achieved in this farmhouse bedroom by papering the walls and slanted ceiling with a small-scale print and corresponding floral pattern. The handsome iron bed is dressed with a white spread, striped pillow, and a striped blanket for chilly nights. A small table acts as a bedside stand and allows space for a kerosene-style lamp with a white glass shade. In keeping with the room's decor, the window treatment is decorative, incorporating a formal striped Roman shade, while select accessories such as meadow flowers and a variety of framed prints add quirky finishing touches.

colors. Blue and white is a farmhouse country favorite, but reds, greens, or even white can take center stage. Paint is the least expensive way to set the tone, though a scrubbable wallpaper in stripes or a cheerful mini print has strong country appeal.

With the numerous flooring options available today you can select the appropriate material to meet your individual needs. Hardwood and wide plank flooring are definitely country style, but resilient flooring is available in so many colors and patterns that you may opt for its easy-care convenience. Consider a subtle striped floor or a checkered pattern—there's even resilient flooring available with the look of old linoleum. Tile can also be used, perhaps in a country color or a rustic terra-cotta.

The Farmhouse Kitchen and Bathroom

The kitchen is the traditional center of the farmhouse country home. Typically large and roomy with the inviting warmth of a wood-burning stove, the smell of freshly baked bread, and a potpourri of old kitchenware on hand, it's one of the hallmarks of a simple country life. That same intimate spirit can be re-created today by designing a background using your favorite

Above: Color sets the tone in this 1990s interpretation of an American farmhouse kitchen. Bead-board cabinets are painted an attractive muted green to blend with open shelving above the refrigerator and the wall beside the vintage stove. To lighten the room and emphasize its height, the wall space above the cabinets is cream with white trim. Matchstick window shades add natural texture and country appeal. A round table with a blue and white cloth and oak chairs are apt furnishings in this casual, inviting space.

Kitchen cabinets made of oak, knotty pine, or cherry are perfect in a farmhouse setting. They should be fairly simple cabinets with wooden, brass, or iron pulls and little in the way of architectural flair. Glass-front cupboard doors are an appealing way to display dishware provided they're not too formal-looking. Regarding painted cabinetry, white cupboards can create a focal point for a spectacular farmhouse kitchen. Add a butcher block or old farm table as a center island or workstation, and select countertops (wood, tile, or a colored laminate) for convenience as well as country style.

If you have space in the kitchen for a freestanding cupboard, it will go a long way toward contributing to the spirit of farmhouse style. An antique or reproduction pie safe with wire-mesh or punched-tin doors, an old baker's cupboard,

American Graniteware

* Graniteware enamel-covered iron or sheet-steel household goods were made from the late 1800s through the 1930s.

* It was produced in colors such as gray, white, red, cobalt blue, green, lavender, brown, and black.

* Common decorative patterns for graniteware included mottle, swirl, marble, shade, "end of day" (which has three or more colors), and "snow on the mountain" (a lumpy white over a primary color).

* Graniteware was made for kitchen and household use and included items such as pots and pans, utensils, pitchers, muffin pans, pie plates, roasters, teapots, and coffeepots.

* The price of a graniteware piece is generally determined by color, pattern, item, and condition. For example, while cobalt blue and white swirl pieces are costly, plain white with a colored trim is still affordable and readily available for collecting.

Above: A lovely, large-patterned wallpaper creates a fitting atmosphere for this kitchen imbued with farmhouse country spirit. Wood cabinetry is always at home in such a setting, and special touches, such as the stamped copper panel on the refrigerator door, add decorative appeal. A handy wall-hung rack creates out-of-the-way space for a collection of cookware and a display shelf near the ceiling creates ample room for favorite collectibles.

or an early 1900s Hoosier cabinet can be both decorative and practical, providing space for both storage and display. Other furnishings include the farmhouse table and chairs, which can be painted or left with a mellow wood finish.

Accessories in the farmhouse-style kitchen include lighting fixtures such as a metal (preferably iron) chandelier hung above the table and recessed lighting for countertop work areas. Natural lighting from windows can be softened

with lace panels or cheerful curtains in a floral or mini print. Kitchenware that lends itself to display might include old stoneware crocks, baskets, green-glazed or yellowware bowls, vintage utensils, and the colorful graniteware produced from the late 1800s to 1940. The secret to displaying objects in the kitchen is to assemble a grouping that imparts farmhouse country style but doesn't take over the room.

Above left: The antique enameled stove, copper hot-water tank, and old cast-iron sink clearly pay tribute to the past in this quintessential American farmhouse kitchen. Walls have been painted a crisp white to create a spacious feeling and windows are outfitted with matching white sheers. A wood floor imbues the room with rustic charm, while the painted farmhouse table is covered with a spirited red and white cloth. Kitchenware such as yellowware bowls, vintage utensils, and a graniteware bread box add period decorative accents.

Above right: Reminiscent of an old-fashioned country store, this remarkable kitchen calls upon antiques and collectibles to set a decorative tone. A deep shade of green provides a striking backdrop for stoneware crocks, advertising memorabilia, and a beautiful free-standing cabinet with bins for various staples. Metalwork chairs with floral cushions pull up to the laminate-top table and lighting is provided via a brass hanging fixture with lovely blue glass shades.

The bathroom can be given a good infusion of farmhouse country spirit by adding a colorful bead-board wainscot and then painting or papering the area above it. A wood floor can be painted, while a tile or vinyl floor can be decorated with a brightly hued hooked or braided rug. An old-fashioned claw-foot tub would be ideal, and the sink can be encased in a vintage painted or oak cupboard. Add a mason jar filled with fresh wildflowers, a chip-painted chair for stacking towels, and a small hanging cupboard for toiletries. Small framed prints can be hung on the wall, and baskets always come in handy for keeping necessities such as shampoos and soaps nearby.

Above: This farmhouse-inspired bath is a triumph of coordination. Pale blue walls, white trim, and an oak floor create the perfect surroundings for the old-fashioned sink outfitted with gleaming brass hardware and the tub encased in bead-board paneling. By introducing select accessories such as a ladder-back rocking chair, fresh flowers, framed floral prints, a vintage-style lighting fixture, and a rustic mirror, this picture-perfect setting becomes a harmonious tribute to country style.

Chapter Eight

Modern Country

The modern country interpretation of country style is an eclectic approach to a casual decorating scheme. It is especially appealing in a setting where the location or architectural design of a home does not dictate a particular style or nudge you toward specific regional influences. The perfect examples might be a modern suburban home, high-rise apartment, or converted commercial building.

The modern country decorating style is also ideal for those who prefer an almost minimalist approach to outfitting their home, or for those who take great pleasure in bringing seemingly disparate objects together to make a uniquely harmonious whole. Furniture and simple decorative accessories are the focal point of every room, while backgrounds are deliberately understated.

The Scandinavian Influence

The modern approach to country decorating can certainly make use of the furniture styles, antiques, and collectibles discussed in previous chapters, but there are other cultural or period influences that can be introduced into the modern

Above: Blending various objects to create a pleasing country-inspired setting is the "modern" way of doing things. Here, a handsome wood chest with brass pulls showcases antique bisque snow babies that mingle quite happily with a collection of leather-bound books. *Opposite:* This modern country interior pays tribute to Scandinavian design. Light wood tones in the flooring, wood-beamed ceiling, and columns that serve to divide space harmonize with the finely crafted wood furnishings. An ornately carved mantel supports select items, while a grandfather clock continues the theme of bringing the past into the present.

country home as well. For example, in the Scandinavian countries of Norway, Sweden, and Denmark, a style developed at the turn of the century that has influenced country home interior design ever since. To make the most of limited natural lighting and make interiors more cheerful, a palette of soft colors, casual print fabrics, rustic light wood furnishings, and hand-decorated painted finishes on everything from chairs and tables to cupboards and trunks replaced the gloomy interiors of the Victorian age. This was largely the work of one man in Sweden, Carl Larsson, whose hand-drawn renditions of a new country decor appeared in book form almost a century ago. The rest, as they say, is history.

Among the more notable antique furnishings of Scandinavian country style are the beautiful furniture pieces ornamented with rosemaling, or fanciful

painted designs. Such folk art pieces were lovingly embellished with floral motifs, painted stripes or scrolls, and sayings, and while vintage examples may be quite scarce and expensive, modern renditions are being crafted today by Americans of Scandinavian ancestry. Consider the serene, absolute beauty of a cupboard or chairs with rosemaling set against a neutral backdrop in a modern country home.

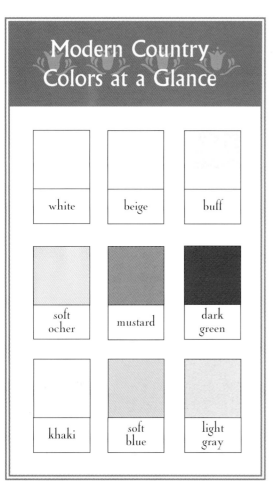

Modern Country Colors at a Glance

white	beige	buff
soft ocher	mustard	dark green
khaki	soft blue	light gray

Other painted furnishings can make a bold or subtle statement in a contemporary country home. Long a staple of American country style, all sorts of handcrafted, painted pieces such as chairs, cupboards, benches, stools, and tables are eagerly sought and cherished for their mellow faded paints and homey designs. The rural craftsmen of the eighteenth and nineteenth centuries often turned to paint not only to protect the wood but to give a piece a uniform appearance, since a combination of local woods may have been used in construction. During the 1700s craftsmen might have adorned a painted

Above: Painted furniture pieces don't have to be primitive to imbue a modern setting with country spirit. Here a 1930s blue and white porcelain enamel-top table and matching chairs are joined by an old Hoosier kitchen cabinet with similar trim.

cupboard with a grained or swirled design that they created with feathers, combs, sponges, or even crinkled paper. At this time such extra efforts were purely to decorate furniture, but by the early nineteenth century graining was done to imitate more costly furniture turned out by cabinetmakers' shops. Along with these imitative pieces, painted country furniture can also be considered plain or imaginative. *Plain* refers to an item painted in a single color with no added embellishment. Popular country colors used on antique and reproduction furniture include red-brown, gray, yellow ocher, mustard, dark green, light green, and variations of blue. In contrast, *imaginative* painting made use of cultural motifs, hand lettering, and anecdotal scenes to personalize and beautify handcrafted furniture pieces.

Today's modern country home is the ideal setting for an enchanting painted cupboard. By introducing such a piece into any room in the home, the ambiance changes: the room suddenly says country in a big way. And while authentic, antique painted furniture is becoming harder to find, skilled artisans are turning their attention to creating excellent reproductions with all the country charm of their vintage counterparts.

The Arts and Crafts Influence

A single design influence such as the Arts and Crafts movement can also have big impact on a modern country home. The honest craftsmanship, clean lines, and satisfying proportions of Arts and Crafts–inspired furnishings or decorative accessories can enliven the spirit of a contemporary country setting. Yes, Arts and Crafts is indeed a highly popular decorating style unto itself, but introducing an element or two of this particular design into a modern home is a striking way to introduce a tribute to the past.

The Arts and Crafts movement began in England and spread to the United States by the late 1800s. It was, in part, a reaction to crowded Victorian interiors and the often inferior furniture being mass-produced during the mid- to late nineteenth century. It was also created in reaction to the overabundance of bric-a-brac on every surface and as such is a style based on simplicity, quality

Above: A variety of cultural, period, or religion-inspired designs can be called upon to fashion a modern country ambiance. Here, Shaker influence contributes notable country charm to this living space where the simplicity of elegant wood tones and quality craftsmanship are used to furnish and decorate. For example, a tape-back Shaker armchair resides alongside a striking chest of drawers with wood pulls and an understated lamp.

period design has seen the L. & J.G. Stickley Company once again turning out the Mission-style furniture associated with this movement. The beautiful rectangular lines of a Mission oak settee or chair can be integrated beautifully into a modern country setting as a salute to the spirited ingenuity at the heart of country style.

Other elements of country decorating—such as Native American crafts, the cultural influences of various other nations, or simply your favorite collection (for example, vintage toys or wooden decoys)—will also enhance a modern country decor. The key aim, however, is casual comfort. Busy backgrounds detract from the simplicity of a modern country setting, so painted walls, hardwood floors, and subtle trim are called for. Upholstered furnishings in easy-care fabrics should be roomy and inviting enough for an afternoon nap. Additional seating pieces should be solid and comfy, not dainty and fragile. Tables should be large enough to accommodate a group of family and friends for a casual country meal, and bookcases or built-in shelves mean less clutter scattered about the room. Windows let the outdoors in; light is filtered through shutters or shades. In short, modern country is a well-edited, comfortable blend of the old and the new—a highly personal approach to furnishing a home to meet your individual lifestyle.

craftsmanship, and straightforward furniture designs. Much of the handcrafted (and later machine-made) furniture was made from oak, and decorative accessories included striking metalwork, leatherwork, pottery, hand-embroidered linens, and fabrics with stylized nature motifs. Again, antique pieces may be costly depending on their quality, but renewed interest in this particular

Above: Thanks to simple white walls and window shades, furnishings are allowed to take center stage in this modern country living room. Comfy and contemporary upholstered furnishings are blended with a Mission oak rocker, a product of the Arts and Crafts movement. The rocker has been updated with plump white cushions and a patriotic toss pillow that provides a traditional accent. By including a plaid throw, fresh flowers, and a few well-edited accessories, this room has all the comforts of a true country home.

The Modern Entryway

For starters, the entryway in a modern country home should meet your basic needs without creating excess. Ambiance can be introduced by painting walls white, a pale neutral shade, or a creamy white with just a hint of blue, pink, or green. Trimwork can have a pale wood finish or be painted white.

Floors in the entryway should be practical. Tile, brick, or slate are hard-wearing and easy to maintain. If a hardwood floor is preferred it should have a protective finish, and a tray should be handy for footwear. A hand-loomed carpet runner (something with stripes or checks) can be used to help protect the floor.

Carefully selected furnishings and accessories in the entryway tell visitors that your home is designed around the country premise that utilitarian items work best. A brass coat tree can provide the perfect resting spot for coats. Add a honey pine table for packages and mail, and perhaps a Windsor chair. In a small space, hooks on the wall and a painted bench or an Arts and Crafts settee may be all that's called for. Accessories can be limited to a select few: an overhead lighting fixture with a white glass globe, a single piece of artwork on an entryway wall, and perhaps a crystal or smoky black vase filled with an arrangement of simple flowers.

Open living spaces are especially adaptable to a modern country decorating scheme. Whether home is a converted barn, an old house where walls have been removed in favor of a single, large space, or a contemporary dwelling with a sizable great room, the areas where you truly do most of your living can flow effortlessly into each other with spectacular country style. A high, wood-beamed ceiling, a vaulted ceiling, or a series of painted support posts serving as a contemporary room divider can help set the stage for a casual and modern country-style interior.

Above: This serene entryway is a perfect example of how less can be more in a contemporary country setting. Massive timbers, cream-colored walls, and pine flooring play host to a pair of beautiful Windsor chairs, a country-style bench with heart cut-outs, and a colorful area rug. The large, luminous window has been left bare, in keeping with the spare aesthetic of the space, while a simple ceiling fixture provides overhead light.

The Modern Living Room and Dining Room

Walls in the modern living room and dining room look their best when painted some variation of white, or one of the new pale earth tones. Pastels can also be used: for a simple but decorative touch, walls can be wood-paneled on the bottom third of the wall (paneling looks spectacular painted white) and then a soft hue can be selected to paint the rest of the wall space. Architectural embellishment should be more rustic than refined—wood beams, large windows, and a handsome fireplace with a simple wood mantel will do quite nicely.

Wood floors in the modern country living room and dining room will impart a casual country spirit. Polished hardwood flooring is striking on its own but can be accessorized with an area rug with stripes, geometric patterns, a Native American design, or a stylized floral motif reminiscent of the Arts and Crafts movement. An Oriental rug can also be a wonderful addition to a modern country decor, adding both color and timeless elegance. Wide plank flooring, especially when it wears the soft gold patina acquired over time, needs little in the way of accessories. Use an area rug to define specific locations if you must but allow the beauty of the aged floor to speak amply for itself.

Windows in the living and dining rooms can be left bare when privacy is not a concern or there's no need to filter direct sunlight (as with a northern exposure). When a window dressing is required or preferred, consider fabric shades, wood shutters (painted crisp white to match woodwork or walls), or fabric or vinyl blinds. A visit to a specialty shop is definitely called for given the myriad choices when it comes to these no-nonsense window covers. For example, horizontal blinds are available in assorted colors and with slats of different widths. Vertical blinds are also available and a popular choice for sliding glass doors or a bank of windows. When it comes to fabric shades, a

Above: Set off against a white background, treasured pieces bring timeless appeal and traditional charm to this living room. An heirloom Victorian rocker is accompanied by a table just large enough to hold a favorite stash of books, and a lovely basket and striped runner infuse the setting with country colors and textures. Opposite: Colorful farmhouse accents bring a dash of old-fashioned style to a modern country living room. Beautiful, slipcovered easy chairs are accessorized with comfy pillows wearing checks and stripes, while the plump sofa sports a patchwork quilt for curling up. A rustic, chip-painted bench finds new life as a coffee table and allows a spot for a twig planter filled with tiny blooms. Note, too, the pair of candlesticks and the candlestick lamp on the round table—they add a hint of romantic charm.

Roman or pleated shade will blend nicely in a modern country setting while an Austrian shade would be much too fussy. Fabric shades can be custom-made in everything from a checkered linen to light-filtering organza.

Furniture and decorative accessories in the modern country living room are a matter of personal choice. With solid comfort and convenience your primary concern, you'll need the perfect sofa and easy chairs. When you shop, by all means try them out. A large sofa and chairs with big rolled arms and deep cushions or modular seating are only two of many possibilities. Select light-colored fabrics that are long-wearing and easy-care and that convey a casual spirit. Striped ticking, linen canvas, or tweed are good choices; make sure the fabric has been treated to a soil- and stain-resistant finish.

Left: This picture-perfect living space has spectacular views inside as well as out, thanks to the architectural design of the windows. By incorporating built-in shelves as wall space, favorite country items can be displayed without causing clutter. With a rocking chair positioned close by, treasured books are within easy reach while miniature wooden boxes, a brass nautical lamp, and binoculars add an old-fashioned yet personal touch to a lovely modern scene.

Other furnishings in the living room might include wicker tables and chairs, glass-top tables, or warm wood tables and assorted chairs. By incorporating a wall of shelves you can create out-of-the-way space for a television, a VCR, stereo equipment, books, and collectibles. A freestanding entertainment center can serve the same purpose, as can an armoire or a large antique dresser. If using a vintage piece, be sure not to ruin it by making holes or otherwise destroying its integrity.

Decorative accessories and country collectibles in the living room naturally include lamps or lighting fixtures. Go modern with track lighting or recessed lighting combined with table lamps, or give the room a touch of old-fashioned style by making your lighting a focal point—an Arts and Crafts metalwork lamp, perhaps? Other decorative touches that hint at country style include baskets, wood carvings, vintage signs, folk art pieces, and various textiles. When planning decorative elements for a modern country setting remember that less is more, so select pieces carefully and choose things you love. For example, a striking patchwork quilt can become a work of art when showcased on a living room wall. A vintage general store, camp,

Right: French doors, perhaps leading out to a sunporch, have been opened wide to celebrate spring and a casual family brunch. Country spirit is evident in the details—a wood table covered with a vintage cloth and ladder-back chairs painted white. A simple bouquet and potted geraniums add color and a touch of the outdoors. Last but not least, the black-and-white-checkered floor runner contributes a dash of contemporary country to a modern setting.

The Elements of Modern Country Style

❋ Open living spaces and architectural elements such as beams, posts, and large windows

❋ Comfortable upholstered furnishings with easy-care fabrics in solids, stripes, or checks

❋ Accent furnishings in light wood tones, wicker, or white painted finishes

❋ Antique furniture pieces (or reproductions) such as cupboards, benches, tables, and chairs

❋ Minimal window dressings including fabric shades, shutters, and vinyl blinds

❋ Well-edited collections with a country theme such as folk art pieces, baskets, and pottery

Above: This modern country dining room features rugged architectural elements that show furnishings to their best advantage. By keeping it simple, the light wood table and Windsor chairs become a focal point. The oval braided rug defines space and adds rich color. Sideboards flanking a doorway and metal wall sconces add balance and symmetry. The windows are left bare to enhance lovely views and an iron chandelier adds crafted flair and nighttime ambiance.

or advertising sign can claim a place of honor above the mantel. A one-of-a-kind folk art piece can become a focal point on a fireplace mantel or shelf. The goal is a relaxed, uncluttered, and comfortable setting that combines modern comfort with a notable country slant.

The dining room can be strikingly beautiful when outfitted simply. Juxtapose an antique harvest table with the modern lines of metal chairs, or surround a glass-top table with a set of Windsor chairs or Mission oak chairs with embroidered cushions. A chip-painted table will clearly convey country style; when accompanied by upholstered slipper chairs it becomes a visual delight. The possibilities are endless, but be sure to look for tables and chairs that say function, not fancy. Other furnishings that may prove useful in the modern dining room include a cupboard or cabinet for displaying pottery or a buffet table that serves as the resting spot for a potted plant or lovely piece of architectural salvage. All it takes is a bit of imagination.

To complete the dining room add a light fixture above the table—something that either blends into the background or steals center stage with its definite country charm. You may wish to add a piece of artwork, a framed sampler, or a series of smaller prints to a dining room wall. A vase of fresh flowers or pottery bowl filled with fresh fruit atop the table is the ideal finishing touch.

Above: This contemporary home with its play of ceiling heights and an open floor plan exudes country style. Wood timbers and a golden wood floor add natural texture. In the dining area, an antique table dressed with a checkered cloth is joined by matching oak chairs. A simple wooden bowl filled with fruit makes an inviting centerpiece, and a geometric patchwork quilt becomes modern art for the wall.

The Modern Bedroom

The bedroom in the modern country setting combines welcome comfort with minimal fuss. Painted walls, in your favorite soft or neutral hue, and a wood floor make a natural backdrop. In the bedroom especially, you'll want to add a rug for comfort. Consider a hand-loomed rug with a graphic design, a rug with a geometric motif, or maybe a needlepoint rug with a spray of flowers that recalls a country garden.

Your options in regard to a window treatment are equally numerous. White or color-coordinated fabric or vinyl blinds, fabric shades, or shutters are best for a simplified style. Any of these are ideal in the bedroom; their sleek lines serve to control natural light while blending effortlessly into an unassuming background. If, however, you'd like your window dressing to add a pretty element of country to the bedroom, lace panels are a nice contrast to modern furnishings and add softness and old-fashioned appeal.

Furnishings for the bedroom naturally include the focal point—the bed. When the bed is placed against a wall of built-in shelving, you can often do without a headboard and can use a quilt and perhaps lace pillowcases to imbue

Above: Little is needed in the way of decorative accessories when you have such a breathtaking view. This cozy attic bedroom features a creamy color palette and golden plank flooring as a subtle background for a quilt-covered bed and homey wicker rocking chair. Windows are left bare to maximize scenic views but note, too, how the windows are themselves decorative in their design. Built-in shelves and cupboard-like drawers keep necessities neatly tucked away.

Opposite: This one-of-a-kind bedroom conveys Scandinavian country style in a thoroughly modern setting. A peaked ceiling and generous use of wood everywhere are complemented by custom-crafted built-in beds. Decorative woodwork, built-in drawer space, and a rich shade of blue paint make this cozy sleep area a visual delight. Blue-striped bedding and a blue and white area rug reinforce the country color scheme.

the room with marked country style. Other signature touches include recycled architectural salvage used as an unusual headboard—let a vintage mantel, or gingerbread trim long since removed from its original perch find new life in an imaginative indoor setting. Of course the bed can always be an heirloom style, such as a beautiful brass or iron bedstead that clearly pulls the past into the present day. And don't forget that color and paint can work magic. A tall four-poster bedstead with a simple white painted finish is a modern take on a decidedly country furnishing.

Above left: *This attic bedroom retreat conveys modern country charm by limiting furnishings and accessories to a select few. A handsome iron bedstead is set against a rustic backdrop and is dressed with no-fuss linens for comfort and practicality. Metal candlesticks on the floor make unexpected decorative accessories, blending effortlessly with the texture of the bedstead.*

Above right: *Creamy yellow walls and billowing white curtains on simple metal rods make eye-catching complements to a lovely pine cupboard in this modern country bedroom. A piece such as this tames clutter and gives the bedroom a crisp, clean look. Stacking baskets on top and adding a bouquet of tulips contributes to the room's relaxed appeal.*

Other pieces in the bedroom include chests of drawers or dressers for storage, which can either be contemporary reproductions or true antiques. A modern country bedroom can be the ideal setting for a beautiful golden oak chest of drawers or a painted piece of cottage furniture. Even the most state-of-the-art bedroom will convey country roots with the introduction of a hand-painted chest placed at the foot of the bed or a rustic willow chair taking up residence in a cozy corner. Decorative accessories in the modern country bedroom should be limited to a select few. A pair of framed architectural prints might grace a wall, a potted tree can reside by a sunny window, or perhaps a twig table can serve as a bedside stand and the perfect resting spot for a metal lamp and a stack of favorite books. And speaking of lamps, why not try something different in the modern country bedroom? Imagine the beautiful simplicity of a bedroom with pale slate-blue walls, an antique wooden sleigh bed, and black metal lamps sporting black fabric shades. Add a print with a black frame and a slipper chair with striped upholstery in white and slate blue. Simplicity is the essence of modern country style, and this decorative concept combined with your own good taste should result in a bedroom that is a pure and absolute pleasure to relax in.

The Modern Kitchen

The kitchen in a modern country setting is a no-fuss utilitarian room that can be both practical and pleasing. Just because it is functional doesn't mean you can't linger or that it is not warm and inviting. For example, follow through with a white or neutral color scheme on walls. For flooring, consider wood, tile, or resilient vinyl flooring, which can offer the look of tile or even old brick at a lower cost.

In the kitchen, cabinetry is an essential design element. A modern country decorating scheme calls for white or light wood tones to impart a casual style. Cupboards have solid or glass-front doors and come in a wide range of styles. Simple and plain works best, with wood or metal pulls and little in the way of architectural embellishment. Imagine the modern country kitchen complete with white cabinets sporting brass pulls, a hardwood floor and countertop, and a professional stainless steel stove—very up-to-date, yet by introducing a wood

Above: *Thoroughly contemporary and efficient and yet warm with country style, this kitchen is no doubt the heart of the home. White cabinetry (some with glass-front doors), an attractive tile backsplash, and rustic plank flooring contribute a timeless quality. A large, restaurant-style stove is a decidedly modern addition that blends in quite nicely. The sink area is designed as a part of the handsome island, which also allows space for casual meals. Select kitchen necessities on display and the ceiling rack with dried flowers are delicate tributes to the past.*

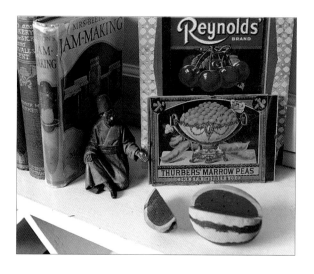

Painted Country Furniture

❀ Look for cupboards, dry sinks, pie safes, jelly cupboards, chimney cupboards, stools, tables, benches, blanket boxes, and washstands.

❀ Many painted pieces available today were handcrafted during the late 1800s and early 1900s.

❀ Examine painted furniture carefully to determine an authentic finish. Antique pieces do not typically feature paint on drawer bottoms and sides, on backs, and underneath trim skirts.

❀ An authentic old paint finish has a patina acquired over time and may be chipped or crazed in areas and show wear spots from use.

❀ Reproduction painted pieces are available and make a fine addition to a country home provided the buyer knows the piece is a reproduction; ideally it should be marked in some way.

❀ The item itself, its age, the quality of construction, and the painted finish will determine pricing. Step-back cupboards and other cupboard forms are in high demand and more costly than a variety of other painted pieces.

floor and countertop you've injected the room with country warmth. In contrast, cabinets can also recall period style, as in a kitchen outfitted with light wood cabinets in an Arts and Crafts style. Combine these with a marble countertop and you've got a hardworking modern kitchen with noteworthy country roots.

Countertops are available in a wide range of materials including tile, wood, marble, stainless steel, and state-of-the-art laminates. Make your selection based on your needs and your budget, for some materials (such as marble) can be quite costly. Tile and laminates are available in a rainbow of colors, although even a basic white can have dramatic impact in a modern country kitchen. For a somewhat tempered but spirited use of tile, make a bold country statement by creating a decorative tiled design in a select area, such as behind the stove or as a backsplash.

Windows in the kitchen should be left bare if at all possible or outfitted with shutters or vinyl mini blinds. Lighting—whether natural or artificial—is

Above: Even a small display or collection can have big impact in a modern country kitchen. Here, colorful advertising memorabilia are combined with a miniature wooden fruit, a ceramic figurine, and a grouping of vintage cookbooks. Opposite: Utilitarian and at the same time strongly reminiscent of kitchens past, this striking kitchen has plenty of country charm. White cabinetry and a wood floor provide classic foundations on which to build. By adding an enamel-top kitchen table and casual chairs, a vintage cookstove, and a few well-chosen accessories—an old-fashioned lighting fixture, red and white tablecloth, and iron pans displayed on the wall—this contemporary country kitchen is complete.

Above: An old-fashioned claw-foot tub infuses this modern bath with a hearty helping of country spirit. Tiles are artistically arranged to create a practical and decorative background. Sometimes just a few imaginatively selected elements can evoke the essence of a style.

important in the kitchen, so combine sunlight streaming through windows or French doors with track lighting, recessed lighting, or hanging pendant fixtures. An iron or brass chandelier can always be situated above a table for a charming accent.

Decorative accessories in the modern country kitchen can be both practical and beautiful. A rack suspended from the ceiling can be used to hang gleaming copper pots and pans, and the space on top of wall-hung cabinets can be the perfect spot for baskets, ceramics, or large pottery bowls that are used on occasion. Recessed shelving built into a kitchen wall can be put to use for stacking cookbooks and vintage kitchenware items; an antique or reproduction step-back cupboard, pine dresser, or old Hoosier cabinet can be used in much the same way. Keep in mind that a small, select grouping of pottery, stoneware jugs, or baskets will impart strong country spirit. It's quality, not quantity, that counts in a modern country setting.

The Modern Bathroom

The bathroom can be a wonderful place to relax and renew your spirits. An inviting tub, a spacious shower, and necessities close at hand can make the private time spent in the bath an indulgence to look forward to. The modern country bath can be all this and more with a few well-chosen decorative techniques that combine high-tech function with down-home charm.

Begin with a white or neutral backdrop and an easy-care floor of tile, resilient flooring, or wood treated with a protective finish. A lovely pedestal sink—substantial, not small and dainty—will impart old-fashioned, timeless style. Hang a gilt-framed mirror above the sink, or choose a mirror with white trim. A claw-foot tub is reminiscent of an early-twentieth-century bath and naturally has a lot of country charm, but a contemporary model can be every bit as stylish with a wood surround or tile trim with a splashy checkerboard design. Black and white, red and white, or blue and white checkered patterns can be used in small doses to endow the room with country spirit.

Accessories in the modern country bath include plush towels stacked and ready, toiletries nearby on a chip-painted or stainless steel shelf, sconces flanking the mirror, and an overhead fixture for stronger general light. Keep bric-a-brac to a minimum—plain and simple says it with style. A small bud vase filled with a single rose, one special print on a bathroom wall, and a candlestick for late-night soaks are enough—fill the tub and enjoy!

Left: Country accessories can be called into use to give a modern bath decorative appeal. This woven basket perched atop a rustic stool is ideal for keeping necessities close at hand. *Above:* A stripped-down approach in this attractive modern bath manages to evoke a strong sense of country style by a selection of fixtures with timeless appeal. A handsome pedestal sink with old-fashioned taps joins a vintage-style tub. A simple wood floor, sheer white curtains, and soft colors allow the fixtures to claim center stage. A small stool and rag rug have been added for good country measure.

Sources

Decorative Accessories

Adirondack Country Store
252 North Main Street
P.O. Box 210
Northville, NY 12134
(800) 566-6235
Assorted accessories for the rustic
home or camp. Call for brochure.

The Chuctanunda Antique Company
One Fourth Avenue
Amsterdam, NY 12010
(518) 834-3983
Specializes in antique French and
European enameled ware. Can be
seen at major antiques shows and does
an extensive mail-order business.
Call for a free brochure.

Country Curtains
The Red Lion Inn
Stockbridge, MA 01262
(800) 876-6123
Country curtains available
by mail-order. Call for catalogue or
visit one of their locations.

The Country House
805 East Main Street
Salisbury, MD 21801
Specializes in samplers, tinware,
crocks, and other decorative country
items. Write for catalogue ($3).

Country Tinware
RR 1, Box 73
Mt. Pleasant Mills, PA 17853
(800) 800-4846
Assorted candleholders, wall sconces,
and lanterns. Call for catalogue.

Covered Bridge Quilt Supply
P.O. Box 333
Winterset, IA 50273
(515) 462-1020
Specializes in reproduction fabrics
for quilts.

French Country Living
10205 Colvin Run Road
Great Falls, VA 22066
(703) 759-2245
(800) 485-1302 (to request catalogue)
Specializes in French country–style
decorative accessories.

Heritage Lantern
25 Yarmouth Crossing Drive
Yarmouth, ME 04096
(800) 648-4449
Specializes in wall and ceiling lights,
sconces, and chandeliers.
Call for catalogue.

Laura Ashley Home Collection
1300 MacArthur Boulevard
Mahwah, NJ 07430
(800) 223-6917
Specializes in fabrics and wallpapers.

Rejuvenation Lamp & Fixture Company
1100 S.E. Grand Avenue
Portland, OR 97214
(503) 231-1900
Deals in reproduction lighting such as
chandeliers, sconces, porch lights, Arts
and Crafts fixtures, and Victorian-era
lighting fixtures.

Renovator's
P.O. Box 2515
Conway, NH 03818
(800) 659-0203
Specializes in lighting, bath fixtures, and
decorative items. Call for catalogue.

Royal Design Studio
386 East H Street
Suite 209-188
Chula Vista, CA 91910
(800) 747-9767
Specializes in stencils.

Arthur Sanderson and Sons, Ltd.
979 Third Avenue
New York, NY 10022
(212) 319-7220
Specializes in wallpaper.

Stulb's Old Village Paint
P.O. Box 1030
Fort Washington, PA 19034
(215) 654-1770
Deals in vintage paint colors for
furniture, walls, and woodwork.

Thibaut
480 Frelinghuysen Avenue
Newark, NJ 07114
(800) 223-0704
Specializes in wallpaper. Call for
availability in your area.

Yowler & Shepps Stencils
3529 Main Street
Conestoga, PA 17516
(717) 872-2820
Specializes in decorative stencils.

Flooring/Rugs

ABC Carpet & Home
888 Broadway
New York, NY 10010
(212) 674-1144

American Olean
1000 Cannon Avenue
Lannsdale, PA 19446
(215) 855-1111

Armstrong World Industries
P.O. Box 8022
Plymouth, MI 48170
(734) 331-7320

Bruce Hardwood Floors
16803 Dallas Parkway
Dallas, TX 75245
(800) 722-4647

Fredericksburg Rugs
P.O. Box 649
Fredericksburg, TX 78624
Specializes in rug hooking kits.
Write for information.

Charles W. Jacobsen, Inc.
401 North Salina Street
Syracuse, NY 13203
Write for free brochure on Oriental rugs.

Karastan Carpets
P.O. Box 12070
Calhoun, GA 30703
(800) 234-1120

Mannington Resilient Floors
P.O. Box 30
Salen, NJ 08079
(609) 935-3000

Yankee Pride
29 Parkside Circle
Braintree, MA 02184
(800) 848-7610
Specializes in hand-hooked rugs.

Furniture

Baker Furniture
P.O. Box 1887
Grand Rapids, MI 49501
(800) 592-2537
Call for nearest dealer.

Broyhill Furniture Industries, Inc.
One Broyhill Park
Lenoir, NC 28633
(800) 327-6944

Century Furniture
Box 608
Hickory, NC 28603
(800) 867-0510
Call for brochure.

Cohasset Colonials
10 Churchill Road
Hingham, MA 02043
(800) 288-2389
Specializes in reproduction Colonial furniture, assembled or in kit form. Call for catalogue information.

Drexel Heritage
101 North Main Street
Drexel, NC 28619
(800) 916-1986

Grange Furniture, Inc.
200 Lexington Avenue
New York, NY 10016
(800) GRANGE-1
Call for dealer locations.

Harden Furniture
8550 Mill Pond Way
McConnellsville, NY 13401
(315) 245-1000
Write for brochure.

LaLune Collection
930 East Burleigh
Milwaukee, WI 53212
(414) 263-5300
Specializes in handcrafted willow furniture.

Maine Cottage Furniture Inc.
P.O. Box 935
Yarmouth, ME 04096
(207) 846-1430

Old Hickory Furniture
403 South Noble Street
Shelbyville, IN 46176
(800) 232-2275
Specializes in rustic furniture.

Palecek
P.O. Box 225
Richmond, CA 94808
(800) 274-7730
Specializes in bamboo, wicker, and rattan furnishings.

Charles P. Rodgers
899 First Avenue
New York, NY 10003
(800) 272-7726
Specializes in brass and iron beds.

Shaker Workshops
P.O. Box 8001
Ashburnham, MA 01430
Specializes in reproduction Shaker furnishings, assembled or in kit form. Write for catalogue.

L. & J.G. Stickley Company
P.O. Box 480
Manlius, NY 13104
(315) 682-5500
Specializes in Arts and Crafts furnishings.

Wellington's Leather Furniture
P.O. Box 1849
Blowing Rock, NC 28605
(800) 262-1049

Yield House
P.O. Box 2525
Conway, NH 03818
(800) 659-0206

Kitchens and Baths

AGA Cookers
P.O. Box 213
Stowe, VT 05672
Write for information.

Crownpoint Cabinetry
153 Charlestown Road
P.O. Box 1560
Claremont, NH 03743
(800) 999-4994

Kohler Company
444 Highland Drive
Kohler, WI 53044
(800) 4-KOHLER

KraftMaid
16052 Industrial Parkway
Middlefield, OH 44062
(800) 654-3308

Moen, Inc.
25300 Al Moen Drive
North Olmsted, OH 44070
(216) 962-2000

Plain & Fancy Custom Cabinetry
Box 519
Schafferstown, PA 17088
(717) 949-6571

Smallbone
A&D Building
150 East 58th Street
New York, NY 10155
(212) 935-3222

Living History Museums

Canterbury Shaker Village
288 Shaker Road
Canterbury, NH 03224
(603) 783-9511

Colonial Williamsburg Foundation
P.O. Box 1776
Williamsburg, VA 23187
(804) 229-1000

Hancock Shaker Village
P.O. Box 898
Pittsfield, MA 01202
(413) 443-0188

Old Sturbridge Village
One Old Sturbridge Village Road
Sturbridge, MA 01566
(508) 347-3362

Shaker Village of Pleasant Hill
3500 Lexington Road
Harrodsburg, KY 40330
(606) 734-5411

Index

Photography Credits

©**Richard Day/Daybreak Imagery:** pp. 75, 86

Envision: ©Melabee Miller: pp. 20, 84, 149 left; ©George Mattei; pp. 31, 152; ©Jean Higgins: p. 85

©**Michael Garland:** pp. 57 (Design by Lauren Elia), 64 right (Design by Gold), 67 (Design by Betty Gould), 100, 107 (Design by Lauren Elia), 108 both, 149 right (Design by Peggy Butcher), 156 (Design by Melanie Mayron)

©**Tria Giovan:** pp. 2-3 (Design by Charles Riley-New York), 5 (Design by Charles Riley-New York), 19, 21, 26, 28 (Design by Charles Riley-New York), 32, 33, 43, 45, 46, 47, 51, 54, 58, 63, 66 both, 69, 72, 91 (Design by Michael Foster-New York), 93 left, 95 left, 97, 101 both, 103, 104, 109, 114 right (Design by Charles Riley-New York), 118, 121, 133, 147 (Design by Charles Riley-New York), 158, 159, 160 (Architecture by Lymon Perry Architects-Berwyn, PA), 166 right (Design by Michele Micheals-Brooklyn, NY), 168 right, 171 left

©**Nancy Hill:** pp. 90, 95 right (Floral Design by Katie Lee), 96 left (Floral Design by Matney Floral Design), 96 right (Photo courtesy of House Beautiful's Home Remodeling & Decorating Magazine), 144 right (Design by Kitchens by Deane), 150 right, 151 (Design by Stirling Design Associates), 167 (Design by Kitchens by Deane),

168 left, 169 (Design by Kitchens by Deane)

INSIDE: ©G. Bouchet: pp. 34, 44 left, 48; ©J. Callaut: pp. 35, 102; ©Y. Duronsoy: pp. 36, 39, 41; ©S. Varenne: p. 37 right; ©J. P. Godeaut: pp. 38, 40, 42; ©L. L. Sullivan: p. 44 right; ©C. Sarramon: pp. 49, 53 left, 170; ©J. F. Jaussaud: p. 50; ©A. Rodier: p. 53 right

The Interior Archive: ©Brian Harrison: pp. 9, 119, 124, 126 right, 129; ©Chris Drake: pp. 13, 93 right, 110, 113, 116 left, 120 both, 122, 123, 130, 131 right; ©Schulenburg: pp. 112, 114 left, 131 left; ©Tim Beddow: pp. 116 right, 117, 126 left, 127, 128

©**John Kane / Silver Sun Studio:** pp. 14, 125

©**image / dennis krukowski:** pp. 29 (Design by David Webster & Associates), 55 (Faraway Ranch), 132 (Design by Richard Byrd), 138 left (Design by Robert L. Zion), 138 right (Design by David Webster & Associates), 139 (Design by David Webster & Associates), 140 (Burgess Lea), 141 (Design by Mrs. Greenwood), 142 right (Design by Nancy Mannucci A.S.I.D.), 144 left (Design by Mrs. Greenwood), 145 (Design by Mrs. Greenwood), 146 (Design by Brenda Speight)

©**Robert Perron:** pp. 60 (Noyes/Vogt arcitects), 70 left (Simpson/Stevens house), 71 (Rob Lucero architect), 135

Courtesy of David Pikul / Chuctanunda Antique Co., Amsterdam, NY: p. 52

©**Eric Roth:** pp. 10 (Design by C&J Katz Studio), 15 (Beauport Museum, Gloucester, MA), 22 (Design by Joanna Paulsen), 23 (Design by Mystic Valley Traders), 24 top (Beauport Museum, Gloucester, MA), 37 left (Design by Mimi Packman), 98 (Design by Nancy Eddy, Inc.), 94 (Design courtesy of Domain Home Furnishing), 106 (Design by Sandy Cohane), 111 (Design by Harry Zeltzer), 115 (Design by Elizabeth Speert, Inc.), 137, 154

©**Brian Vanden Brink:** pp. 7 (Rick Poore, Restoration/Builder), 17 both, 18, 24 bottom, 25, 27, 56 (Peter Bohlin, Architect), 59 (Bullock & Co., Log Home Builders), 61 (Bullock & Co., Log Home Builders), 62 (Rob Whitten, Architect), 64 left, 65 (Peter Bohlin, Architect), 68 (Bullock & Co., Log Home Builders), 70 right (Bullock & Co., Log Home Builders), 73 (Rick Poore, Restoration/Builder), 74, 76 (Thomas Moser Cabinet Makers), 77 (Sabbath Day Lake, ME), 78 (John Silverio, Architect), 79 (Rick Poore, Restoration/Builder), 80 left (Olsen House, Cushing, ME), 80 right, 81, 82 (Jane Doggett, Architect), 83 (Rick Poore, Restoration/Builder), 87 left, 87 right (Farnsworth Homestead, Rockland, ME), 88, 89 (Rick Poore, Restoration/Builder), 94 (Susan Thorn, Interior Design), 105 left (Susan Thorn, Interior Design), 105 right, 134 (Castle Tucker, Wiscassett, ME), 142 left, 143, 148 (Jack Silverio, Architect), 150 left, 153, 155

(Centerbrook Architects), 157, 161 (Jane Langmuir, Interior Design), 162 both, 163 (Bob Knight, Architect), 164 (Stephen Blatt, Architect), 165, 166 left (Centerbrook Architects), 171 right

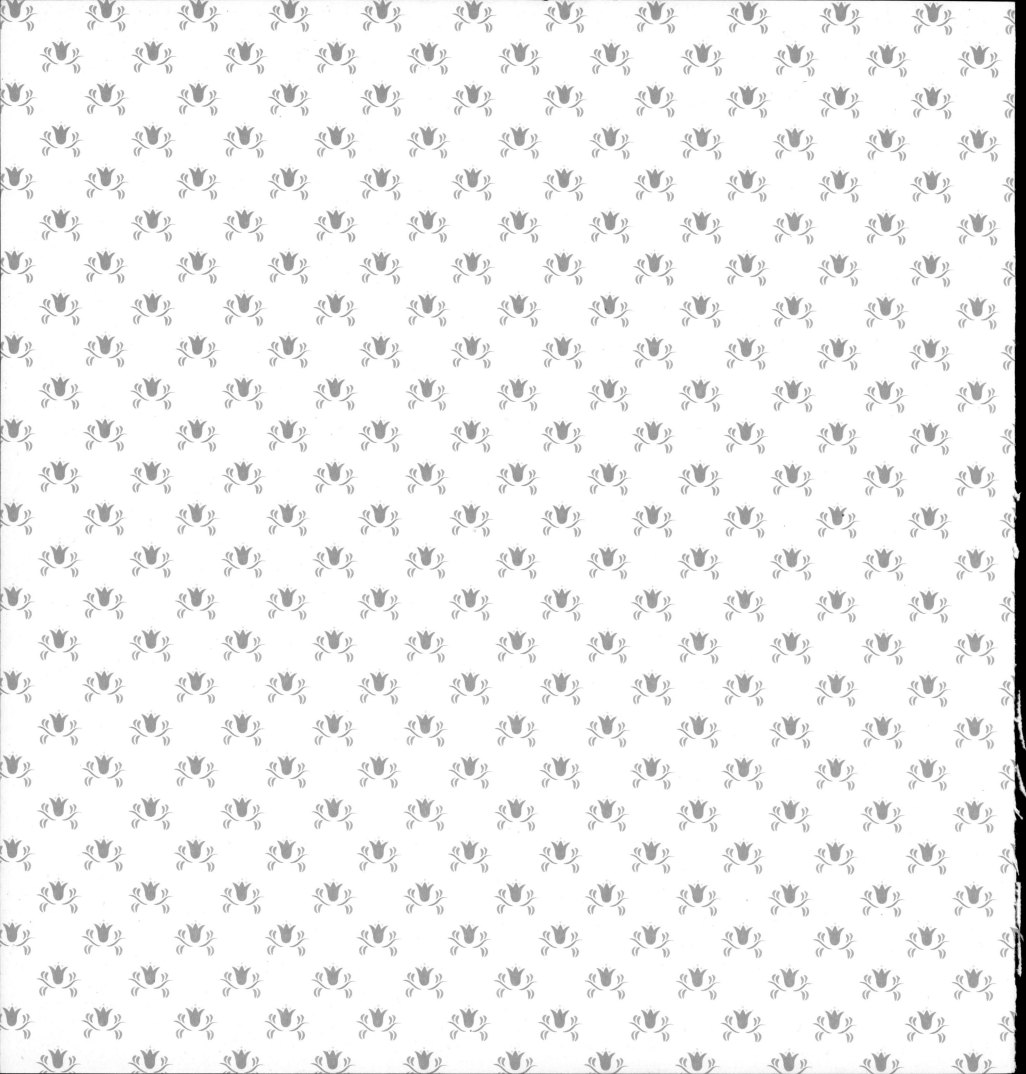